What They Are Saying...

Belinda has a way of showing how painful, life-changing events can bring about a positive outcome. She shares some of her deepest feelings and directs her soulful advice to the readers to be able to change their life once and for all. I felt warmed and inspired by her thoughtful suggestions.

– Dr. Cynthia Quattro
Physician Assistant & Doctor of
Acupuncture & Oriental Medicine

If healing were contagious, you would gladly catch it from Belinda! She is a brilliant and most exuberant light in the face of any challenges that have been presented to her in this lifetime. She will not only help you find your joy as well, but she will hold your hand as you rediscover your soul.

– Robyn Justo
Columnist & Author of "The Expiration Date,"
Contributor to "Kinetics,"
Kathryn and Danion Brinkley's online magazine

Belinda is a master teacher who understands how people shroud their joy. Belinda helped me remove my own back pain through changing how I speak about my body during a healing session a few years ago, so I can attest she truly knows what she's talking about! In "Find your Friggin' Joy" you will gain insights into removing blocks to reprogram your thoughts so that your true light may shine. Learn from Belinda's ancient 'Huna' wisdom and apply her techniques to find happiness.
– Scott Andrews, Founder of AspireNow.com

Belinda Farrell is a rare bright light and a square peg that will never fit into a round hole. That is her gift to us. She helps us discover what it means to really be a human with heart and how to be who you

are – not what others expect you to be. Belinda has lived her words through tough life challenges. Her authenticity and wisdom has made a tremendous difference in my life. She is fierce, compassionate, loving, vulnerable, unapologetic and real. You must read her book.

– Scott Burr
Principal Innovation Consultant, Innovation Scientific, LLC

Every several thousand years, the planet is blessed with a truly remarkable and charismatic presence. A unique individual who has the wisdom and power not only to heal, but also to inspire and motivate others beyond their dreams. Belinda Farrell is one of those rare beings who enriches the soul and warms the heart just by emanating a sheer force of energy. It's undeniable when you meet her. Beneath the impish smile and forever-sparkling eyes, is a woman of unequaled strength and courage, someone who has met the most extraordinary of life challenges and, rather than succumbing to devastating circumstances, rose far beyond them to a singular plateau of grace and achievement. I cannot recommend more highly her personal counseling and her unique life changing knowledge, found in her wonderful products. I have named her Mistress Dolphina, because the age-old dolphins of the seas have clearly selected her as their queen in human form. I, for one, would not argue with the wisdom of these highly evolved creatures, as they have seen more than one species try to dominate the planet. If you have any chance to share the same space with Belinda, move as decisively as possible. If you see a book, CD or DVD from her, spend your last dime. It will surely come back to you many thousands of times!

– David Samson
Author of *The Joy of Depression.*
Media personality, professional speaker

This is a true "medicine book." Reading this visceral and real story of the power of Huna firsthand will liberate you from the plaque of gray, habitual living that entombs our very Life Force and that blocks us from turning setbacks and devastation into empowering opportunities and joy!

- James Wanless, PhD,
Creator *of The Voyager Tarot-Way of the Great Oracle*

Authentic veterans of tough life circumstances rarely can explain the depth of their torment; the pain is too riveting. These same veterans, who have survived and conquered those searing events, cannot always reveal their formulas for success to help the rest of us know how to triumph. Thankfully, Belinda Farrell, one of these authentic conquerors of life's mortifying storms, explains both in her book *Find Your Friggin' Joy*. Belinda unfolds her onslaught of excruciating trials with swift and precise clarity. She then delivers powerful formulas for overcoming excruciating losses, financial ruin, abuse, self-loathing, guilt and personal ruin. She will carry you out of your ruin as she reveals the mysteries of Huna magic and how each of us can heal and resurrect from devastations.

- Dr. Carol Francis
Clinical Psychologist, Marriage, Family & Child Therapist

A gutsy, riveting, easy read from a real-life urban shaman. Do what Belinda says and you too will find your way to the Promised Land … right here and now!

- Shelley Stockwell, PhD
President of the International Hypnosis Federation

I have known Belinda and her profound healing work for several years. I am delighted she has put into words the wonder and wisdom learned through a life path of growth and joy. Allow this book to open your heart and feed your soul. **- Francene Hart**
Visionary artist and author of the *Sacred Geometry Oracle Deck and*
Sacred Geometry Cards for the Visionary Path.

Belinda Farrell is an authentic storyteller who reveals her deepest secrets and shares with us how she courageously faced her inner shadows. Through the power of Huna she shows us how we too can face our inner shadows and find peace and joy. This is a must-read book for anyone who wants to learn how to let go of their old traumas and start living their life in the "precious present."

– Len Suputo, M.D., Board Certified in Internal Medicine, co-author of "A Return to Healing, Radical Health Care Reform and the Future of Medicine"

To Laura —
Be the STAR
that you are —
Aloha
blessings
Belinda
Farrell
2020

FIND YOUR FRIGGIN' JOY

Discover Missing Links from Ancient Hawaiian Teachings to Clean the Plaque of your Soul and Reach Your Higher Self.

BELINDA FARRELL

BALBOA.
PRESS
A DIVISION OF HAY HOUSE

Balboa Press books may be ordered through booksellers or by contacting:

Balboa Press
A Division of Hay House
1663 Liberty Drive
Bloomington, IN 47403
www.balboapress.com
1-(877) 407-4847

Because of the dynamic nature of the Internet, any web addresses or links contained in this book may have changed since publication and may no longer be valid. The views expressed in this work are solely those of the author and do not necessarily reflect the views of the publisher, and the publisher hereby disclaims any responsibility for them.

The author of this book does not dispense medical advice or prescribe the use of any technique as a form of treatment for physical, emotional, or medical problems without the advice of a physician, either directly or indirectly. The intent of the author is only to offer information of a general nature to help you in your quest for emotional and spiritual well-being. In the event you use any of the information in this book for yourself, which is your constitutional right, the author and the publisher assume no responsibility for your actions.

Printed in the United States of America

ISBN: 978-1-4525-6293-3 (sc)
ISBN: 978-1-4525-6295-7 (hc)
ISBN: 978-1-4525-6294-(e)

Four illustrations by Amber Rateike Diaz
Ho'oponopono drawings created at Ram Print, Sausalito, Ca.
Cover and back photographs by Belinda Farrell

Library of Congress Control Number: 2012921250

Balboa Press rev. date: 12/12/2012

CONTENTS

"Forgiveness is the fragrance that the violet sheds on the heel that has crushed it."

~ Mark Twain

THANK YOU TO THOSE RESPONSIBLE FOR THIS BOOK

For years, clients and friends alike have all asked me, "When are you writing your book?"

I knew I had a reason to hold off until now in order to build up enough life lessons. And as I look at it now, I can't think of a better time to release the book than during this intensely critical cleansing process of Humankind, as it breaks down outdated ideas that conflict with the integrity of the Human Spirit.

As I complete the book, I look upon those I must thank. First of all, I thank my fabulous manager for over 15 years, Jennifer Geronimo, who never gave up on the vision of this book. She was always there promoting my CD's and lending her unique originality. On one phone conversation, I happened to say to her, "Just find your friggin' joy." She got so excited and said, "That's the title of your book!" Thank you, Jennifer, for being my confidant and partner throughout this process.

Thankfully, Jennifer introduced me to Jim Ellis, an award-winning writer, editor and organizer. Jim organized and helped edit the book, each chapter and section. Thank you, Jim, for being the ultimate organizer and tightening things up. Your faith in the project carried me through tentative and doubtful times.

Through the sacred lineage of "Daddy Bray," thank you Pila Chiles, for being my "doorway" into higher realms. Your wisdom inspired me to become like you, a "Child of the Rainbow." I am grateful that Hawaii became the crossroads of our connection. You are and continue to be a living inspiration that tells me there is always a new day ... a new beginning.

Heartfelt thanks to my Webmaster of 20 years, Kevin Short, who was sent to me by a "Divine Carrier" when I first put together my site, *HunaHealing.com*. He mainly worked with rap singers before I came along with the themes of ancient healing teachings. He has stuck by me through all these years, and I'll be forever grateful.

Special thanks to my young illustrator, Amber Rateike Diaz, who shows wisdom and talent beyond her years. Her perseverance also came through when her cat peed on several drawings forcing her to make revisions.

Sandy Clementi – you're a gifted soul and computer genius. Thank you for your friendship and patience with my computer skills.

My dearest friend, benefactor and "my person" for over 40 years, Lynn Ober, overcame many fears to accompany me on my first dolphin trip to Hawaii. After reading a chapter I had written in the now out-of-print book, *The Ways of Spirit,* Lynn wrote in her journal that she would pester me until I started writing my own book. "Tell your story and get others to buy it so they can forgive, let go and love unconditionally." Thank you, Lynn, for never giving up on me.

During the days when I was running a little "subpar," my good friend Simant Herkins invited me to see a presentation of the recently released documentary *The Living Matrix* that featured Dr. Eric Pearl demonstrating new modes of healing. Thank you, Simant, for insisting that I attend that event. As a result, after having my Reconnection and several Reconnective Healing sessions, I knew that I MUST finally write this book.

You really never know who your friends are until you're presented with life-altering challenges. Special heartfelt thanks to my close friends Carol and Paul who were "there" for me when I needed supportive friends the most. Carol and I continue to share a deep bond through 35 years of friendship. Our daughters have been best friends since they were two years old. Our weekly walks along Seabright beach are the best! Thank you sincerely for your editorial comments after reading the book---especially that you "get it!"

Many heartfelt thanks to Dawn O'Creene, who took time out of her busy schedule to read the manuscript in its entirety and share her knowledge and valuable counsel for the book.

A warm Mahalo to Randy Peyser, a long-standing dear friend whose sharp wit and seasoned experience in the Literary Field generated fresh ideas for this project.

Thank you to Doug Hackett and Tris Regan for being my first "dolphin tour guides" in Hawaii. I think I made a permanent dent on Doug's arms when he first guided me into the water. I will also forever be grateful to both of you for demonstrating such a beautiful loving partnership.

Celeste Eaton, my dolphin soul sistah – your beauty and grace not only with the dolphins and whales, but with everyone you meet, brings loving inspiration to all of us.

Nancy Rushmer, you give an elegance to aging gracefully and having fun in the moment. As kindred spirits, I'm so honored to call you my friend.

Jim Fox, you were a vital mentor to Brian for which I shall be forever grateful.

Absolute gratitude to God, the dolphins, whales, angels, Hawaiian kumus, my Higher Self, my precious son Brian, who's heart was so open, my loving daughter Jessica, grandson Eddie and son-in-law Edward Lee Brooks Jr.

Thank you to all the people who have touched my life in special ways. That includes you two very special people, Betsy and Tony Andrade. Your smiles and laughter have filled my heart with endless joy.

We have all written this book together.

FOREWORD

A TIME OF GREAT CHANGE is a time for healing ... and a time where sanity must be maintained at all costs. All power, in that time of change, shifts from the complicated, outdated and overriding superpowers, back to the individual. Such an empowered individual is Belinda Farrell. Belinda is a teacher of teachers, with a grace I describe as known only to royalty – a self-made woman whose story is deserving of my Purple Heart. Belinda is human being, the real person of eye contact, who's been there, down in the trenches, "done that."

In this time of greatest change in all history and defining moment, two unique indicators surface, road signs that may help us find our way. 1. A key to the future may lie in the past. 2. That key may have to do with Woman. In the madness may Her healing voice now pierce the veil, and in our darkness soothe, heal and help point the way.

Belinda Farrell is a teacher of the Ancient Ways – the way I call "Hawaiian" – but it is the way shared with Tribal Peoples throughout our world. It is identified as what's simple and what works. They are identified as those who have remained close to our Earth Mother ... those peoples who didn't aspire technologically ... into our madness.

Of recent, there is much argument as to what is real, authentic and of Hawaiian origin, even within the people's own ranks. The anger in that argument is what cost the Hawaiians everything – a male anger that began its reign with the limiting laws of conduct (or "Kapu") of woman. A simple higher reason is the fact that we all have to come through woman to get here ... to experience the earthly realm.

To hear what She has to say is to return to campfire. To experience Belinda live, you would instantly know what I'm talking about. It happens in the moment you hear her healing voice, her incredible Hawaiian chanting. Come now, read, listen, feel her healing words. Tools to your own healing and transformation are within.

Aloha blessings,

– Pila of Hawaii

SECTION 1 – INTRODUCTION

"Nothing in life has any meaning ...
except the meaning that I give it."

– A Course In Miracles

Chapter 1 – "The Magic" – And the Search for the Missing Links

At first, I wasn't going to share a certain chapter of my story. It is vulnerable, painful, raw, and fragile. But then I realized I had to share it for the sake of my healing and potentially your healing. And so I will start here...

On October 16, 2008, I learned that my 30-year-old son committed suicide. I lost my baby boy. He had not been well, living at an Army base in Maryland, suffering with lingering pain in his back, a result of lifelong back struggles originating from a ski injury when he was 12.

Unmotivated to find a job, or fix a computer that had broken, Brian – in the fall of 2008 – was sinking further and further into a hole of financial strife, physical decay and emotional depression. Though I shared with him the ways of healing I had learned over the years in Hawaii – coming back from my own agonizing back issues that had me an invalid in 1992 – Brian was clear he wanted to stay with his Western medicine approach and the medications that had him becoming more and more dependent and distant.

In early October he hadn't answered my calls for days. Deeply disturbed, I called the army base to finally inquire about my son. Detained in the past, I wasn't going to be delayed any longer. I was adamant as the man on the other side of the phone hesitated. I screamed, "You have to go into his room right now!" I waited an excruciating 20 minutes on the phone, just to hear any news. When the man returned, he told me a security officer entered Brian's room and found him on the bed, lifeless. In a hysterical state, I simply collapsed to the floor. I had known Brian was gone, but now it was confirmed. My son was gone.

A few months after losing my son, in January 2009, I got word that I lost all my investment money in a Ponzi scheme. Based on the advice of some trusted friends, I handed over $290,000 from the sale of my mother's house to a Florida investor promising four percent interest each month. By November 2008, checks and communication stopped, and in early 2009 I received a call from a friend who heard the investor and all our investments had disappeared. Of course, I take full responsibility for naively choosing to put "all my eggs in one basket."

The loss of my finances hit hard and rocked my very foundation and sense of security and safety in this world. The loss of my son cannot be measured in any way. Suffice it to say I cannot imagine an agony any deeper.

So, what got me through? What ushered me into a place of acceptance, awareness and peace? It was in a pathway, a teaching, a way of being born in the beauty of ancient Hawaii, and flourishing and finding residence in many societies open to the majesty and the magic of Huna.

Ah yes, the "magic." This chapter is entitled "The Magic" for a reason.

When we see a magician doing a seemingly impossible trick, we define it as "magic" because we do not understand how it works. Right before our eyes something is altered, and it is unexplainable. When it doesn't make sense to our rational mind, it becomes a magic trick. When someone fully heals from an "incurable" disease, we call it a "miracle." To our amazement, such incredible transformations become something outside the realm of logic. Some of the claims of healing in this book may sound "miraculous," but once the techniques are fully revealed, you will understand how it works. At that moment, will it no longer be considered "miraculous" or "magic?" Will the magic disappear; will it be demystified? Will it be just a part of the magic and miracle we all hold within, forever at our access? It is my intention that this book will reveal the magic we all possess to create miracles. You will decide.

What you will find throughout this book can be identified as the "missing links" to fulfilling forgiveness and finding freedom. Sprinkled throughout this text you will discover what has been missing as you attempt to "forgive" that foe, release that pain, and discover that innate joy. It will be a grand journey. And though it may be simple, it may not be easy.

Chapter 2 — Sissies Turn Back

I must be blunt. This book is not for "sissies." Now that may sound judgmental or harsh, but it is said to challenge you at the core level to face what one must face in order to be free. I speak as someone who had to face some of the most painful and debilitating experiences a person must go through: losing a son, losing a fortune, and being completely bed-ridden, unable to walk — a clinical case considered incurable. In order to truly heal my physical disabilities as well as my emotional trauma, I had to take a hard, deep look within myself and see where I had to clear up all negative ties and reform any negative self-perceptions. I had to do some intense research and deep soul searching. Such an inner exploration can be considered scary. A sissy would run away from something scary. This book is not for sissies.

Are you up for the challenge? Can you face any shadows within you in order to be free to find the joy that resides right there where you stand?

If you are unwilling to see what's clogging the depths of your soul, you will have to look elsewhere. This book won't be for you. But if you're sick and tired of doing the same thing over and over and falling in the same hole then I invite you to take a peek at what follows — in these chapters and within the self. I promise, as you do the inner work, and use the tools described within these chapters, you will not only clear what holds you back in life, but also find that friggin' joy that's been locked away for so long!

On my path of healing, the first thing I had to accept — as the principles of the great Huna teachings require — is complete responsibility for all areas of my life. As the strict teachings suggest, I was called to be responsible for everything that happened to me in my life. Everything. I was taught to be the CAUSE rather than the EFFECT, for if I were the cause for creating the events of my life – even unconsciously created – then I also could be responsible for un-creating it.

For example, if I was angry while driving my car and someone else cut me off with the same angry disposition, I would see how I drew that person to me because of my anger. Like a magnet, I would draw angry people towards me if I stayed angry. As I studied my own life, I started to see more examples of this in my everyday world. Becoming conscious of this phenomenon was the first step in changing my behavior. For me personally, fear was my biggest magnet. Whatever frightened me would end up right in front of me, especially around the topic of money.

So how did I remove the fear in my life? For one, I faced it. This is the biggest step in dealing with our invisible barriers. After this, I used the techniques outlined in this book to learn how to move right through the illusions that I had built up. This book will describe in detail the steps to move through fear and any other barrier between you and your joy.

Many of us anticipated 2012, the end of the Mayan Calendar and what some prophets claim to be a more heart-centered reality, in a "New World." In this light, there is a great opportunity to clean out our inner closet from the debris of the past and remove those ancient, stuck, ego-based patterns that no longer serve us or the planet. Without fear, there is only LOVE. Moving forward unafraid, unleashes the power of love. I look forward to the day where we can feel SO PRESENT and AUTHENTIC that we're simply filled with creative ideas and possess the WILL and ENERGY to carry them out.

I don't claim to know all the answers here, but I do feel an obligation to share my journey and the lessons that transformed me from being a scared, fearful child without a voice to the joyful, confident and grateful woman that I am today. We all need to practice "struggling" until we learn the lessons. Even a caterpillar has to struggle in the cocoon to build up the strength in its wings. And when it's ready, the caterpillar cannot help but leave the "old house" behind and burst into a beautiful butterfly. I celebrate all of you, as a caterpillar making its way into a butterfly, on your own journey to fulfilling a promise of power and beauty.

CHAPTER 3 – MY TRANSFORMATIONAL JOURNEY

We all have to start somewhere.

My mother fell in love with an irresistible Irishman, and I was conceived. The marriage only lasted a year and a half, and I never would meet my father. My mother and I lived with my grandparents in Los Angeles. I remember my grandmother walking me to school every day, and my grandfather working nights so he could take me on outings to the park.

My mother worked. Despite the lack of material things, there was plenty of love to go around. I was a curious child and a bit of a daredevil. I definitely did not like to be told what to do, so I would often figure out ways to do the opposite of what was asked. Whenever I heard arguing in the house, I would escape to the rooftops where I had a secret fort under one of the eves. As a daredevil I would love the adrenalin high when jumping from one roof to another.

There were mostly boys in the neighborhood, and that worked out fine for me since I liked playing with the more adventurous kids anyway. We'd climb trees and have bicycle races. I remember rigging up a ramp over three bicycles to perform the "Evel Knievel" jump trick. Luckily, I didn't kill or hurt myself with these stunts. Little did I know that the seeds of these early adventures would later evolve into a stunt-driving career in my 40's.

My family insisted I go to Catholic school – uniform and all – probably to control my rambunctious nature. Obviously, Catholic school and I were not a good mix. I was always getting into trouble with the nuns, whose punishments were formidable. I remember in the third grade being in the confessional telling the priest "my sins" for the week. Expecting him to be thoroughly engaged with my childish crimes, I saw him reading the comics through the hole in the screen. Suddenly it hit me – if he wasn't taking my confession seriously, then neither should I. Thinking of these times, I consider the irony at how much my life would later become so focused on the practice of forgiveness.

At the end of eighth grade I was given my freedom papers and told not to return to Catholic school. It was a polite way of being "expelled." I could not have been happier! Finally attending a public school, I could relax, be myself, and talk to boys without punishment. My ninth grade drama teacher encouraged me to audition for acting roles. Diving into different characters unlocked many trapped emotions within, and I was hooked into the dream of becoming an actress someday. High school years at John Muir High School in Pasadena were opportunities to grow and take risks. Becoming a Song ("pom pom") Girl was a huge accomplishment, despite dancing on a sprained ankle during the finals. during the finals I was dancing on a sprained ankle. Performing the routine, despite the pain, proved to me I could get through anything if I put my heart and soul into it.

I graduated from UC Berkeley in 1966 with a degree in Spanish and English at the height of the Free Speech Movement. The Vietnam War was going strong, and Mario Savio led the protesters on campus. It was a tumultuous time to be a student anywhere. After graduation I was scheduled to attend the Pasadena Playhouse to begin my acting career. However, the Universe had other plans for me. The Playhouse closed down that year for renovations so I continued with my seasonal job at Disneyland. I interviewed to be a tour guide who carried the white flag around the park. Instead I was put into the magical costume of Snow White and chummed around with seven verbally caustic dwarfs. At least the children were entertained. I remember one little girl looking up to me with bright inquiring eyes saying, "I thought you ate the apple and died!" I bent down to reassure her that the Prince kissed me and I woke up.

After Disneyland I secured a temp job at the ABC Network in Hollywood – one step closer to that acting career … or so I thought.

The KABC News Department was down the hall from my office, and I was always making excuses to check out the "breaking news." As fate would have it, the AFTRA (American Federation of Television and Radio Artists) union went on strike and I auditioned to become part of a temporary news crew. We covered both hard and fluffy news. I interviewed Governor Ronald Reagan, numerous actors, a nudist colony, and was even an eyewitness to a robbery and murder crime scene. It turned out that I was comfortable in front of a camera without any formal training. In the late 60's there were few female reporters so I had to work extra hard to prove myself.

While on an assignment, I was spotted by a commercial agent in Hollywood and offered a job. Again, I felt like I was on my way to that acting career. As fate would twist things once again, my life went another way. For the previous year, the CIA had been conducting a Top Security Clearance on me, and it finally came through. Because of my fluency in Spanish, I was recruited to be a covert CIA agent in Madrid, Spain.

There are definitely defining moments in our lives, and this was one of them. I decided to go to Washington D.C. to follow through with CIA protocol instead of staying in Hollywood to pursue a budding acting career. However, after a week at CIA headquarters, it was obvious that the CIA and I were not a comfortable fit. When I see movies today depicting spies getting "bumped off" right and left I feel confident in my decision. At a pivotal moment, I realized during a medical exam, that the CIA had innovative ideas to use my sexuality in order to get certain "classified information from ... men and women." This was a deal-breaker for both of us.

There would have to be other ways to satisfy the urge for travel and adventure. Rather than go back to Hollywood, I stayed in Washington DC and got a job working for Senator Charles H. Percy (R), of Illinois – another defining moment. My short-term press background in LA was enough to get me hired. Three months later, a man named William walked into the office – he would be the man who would become my husband and the father of my two children.

The lessons that come from a marriage with children can go so deep, and bring up so much. What can start out as a fairy tale and the "American Dream" can turn into something else, given each other's path and belief systems. Though my husband, as a physician, provided for his family, he was definitely a man about his career and business, and not his relations with his kids and wife. Though not routinely physically abusive, there was one moment that would forever alter our relationship – as spouses and as a family. In our 13th year of marriage, when asked to help with "potty training" our young son Brian, William snapped and began beating on me. He would never comment on the outburst, but the experience had its lasting effects.

Though I was too scared to leave at the time, I was able to muster enough courage to leave five years later. I realized the lessons over time. I had always been told what to do and who to be in the past; I was a passive person. I had the belief that I had to make someone else happy. Once I had the experience of outright abuse, I had my own awakening and knew I had to grow into a deeper sense of self. I realized:

- I don't need to take abuse. I deserve the best.
- I can do what I need to do, and not just do what I'm told to do.
- I need not be passive, but active and powerful in my reaching for my dreams.
- No one can make another happy. It's our own responsibility.
- You can give someone temporary happiness with gifts, trips, and encouraging words. But true JOY comes from within and your own soul's journey.

After 18 years together, we dissolved the marriage. It was never my intention to be divorced. I wanted to be married forever. But I made the choice when I felt my soul was being compromised and my entire being unrecognized and unfulfilled.

Divorced at 40, my soul's journey went into hyper-speed. My first real teacher was motivational speaker Tony Robbins. After taking the first firewalk (walking on coals at 2,000 degrees) I knew I could learn how to conquer my fears. The firewalk is really a metaphor for what you can do in your life. Knowing that I could walk on fire, I asked myself, "What else would I like to do in my life?"

The answer came. I wanted to drive a racecar. Tony taught us a mantra, "If you CAN'T, you MUST; If you MUST, you WILL." I enrolled in the Bob Bondurant School for High Performance Driving in Sonoma, California. Knowing nothing about racing, I became a "sponge" with this new material. I used to get car sick as a child even looking at a curvy road. I had to get over that hurdle pretty fast. Being in the driver's seat gave me a sense of power. At least I could be in control of a machine, whereas all my life I felt that someone else was controlling me. I felt right at home on the racetrack. Even though I had to learn difficult maneuvers, I could hit my marks with ease. At the end of the 4-day training, I was offered a job driving for Buick and Cadillac in upstate New York. After two weeks of putting 14 cars through their paces amid breathtaking locations – and getting paid for it – I was hooked on professional driving. I attended a rigorous stunt driving course learning how to do forward and backward 180's and 360's, high performance driving and terrorist driving.

My partner Bill Douglas and I started to get hired to do car commercials. Being a member of Screen Actors Guild as an actress and model, stunt driving was added to the resume. We joined a racing team in Los Angeles, and the jobs kept pouring in. As a woman in her 40's, I was a kid at heart finally doing something I loved passionately – taking risks and really feeling alive. No more was I boxed into somebody else's model of what they thought was good for me.

That feeling of unbridled JOY is at the heart of this book. Being true to ourselves gives us a sense of purpose and fulfillment on our soul's journey. When we feel we have "hit the mark" we feel so good inside, much like a hummingbird might feel as it sucks nectar from a flower.

I continued to be fascinated with healing and transforming my fear. Sure, I was fearless driving racecars, but what would help the really deep stuff lurking within? One of my biggest fears was water. I never admitted that fear to anyone, even Tony Robbins. To continue the process of deep inner cleansing, I received training in Hypnotherapy, Neuro-Linguistic Programming, and Past-Life Regression. Ironically, the advanced courses were conducted in Hawaii, a landmass surrounded by water.

While in Hawaii, I was introduced to HUNA, the ancient healing path of the Hawaiians. When I heard the chants, sleeping cells awakened from within. I knew this was the "icing on the cake" for which I was searching. For three years I studied Huna and used the processes for my clients and myself.

Little did I know it would come to save my life. After years of physically pushing my body to its limits, I was faced with a debilitating spinal ailment that forced me to choose between surgery and applying what I had learned to heal myself. It all started with a severe pain in my left hip, which gradually worsened until my legs no longer supported me. I ended up collapsing with herniated discs, nerve damage and paralysis on the left side of my body. I could no longer walk or sit; I could only lie down. Doctors said for me to ever walk again, I needed surgery to correct the damage. Having been married to a doctor for 18 years, I was well aware of the risks of back surgery. I also deeply believed that the body had a healing mechanism that – when given the right direction – can find its way back to wholeness.

Through the techniques I learned through Huna and the techniques outlined in this book, I had one of those "miracles" that only real "magic" can bring. My spine completely aligned itself in four days of intensely focused healing work. Even the scoliosis I was born with disappeared. Because of this amazing healing, I retired from stunt driving and modeling and began teaching Huna and hypnosis full time. I also decided to devote my energy to sharing this information with others ... and this includes you.

Chapter 4 – Why I
Wrote This Book

Writing has never been a passion of mine. My daughter Jessica is the gifted writer in the family. But with the events that took place these last two years, I knew I had to write this book. It's one thing to heal from an illness that happened 15 years ago, but when a sudden emotional storm hits you like a tsunami, as it did for me, then you wonder if all the spiritual survival skills can still apply. They do. As revealed earlier, my only son Brian committed suicide with an overdose of pain medication after struggling for years with back pain and two spinal surgeries. He had just graduated from college with a major in Criminal Justice and also made Sergeant First Class in the Army Reserves. But he could not carry on through his pain. And his loss is my loss. Nothing in life prepares you for losing a child. My grief was beyond comprehension, and emotions still ebb and flow like the tides.

It is said that when it rains, it pours. After the loss of my son, and then the loss of my savings in a Ponzi scheme investment, I felt completely powerless. Reeling from the death of my son, it took me several weeks to face the reality of also having my income cut. I reminded myself of my spiritual core and had to stay positive to do the healing processes. There was no time to feel sorry for myself. I had to be courageous and face the harsh reality.

I sold what I had in order to live. Thankfully, I went to live with my daughter, son-in-law and grandson, taking over the childcare to pay my portion of the rent. I would find peace of mind thanks to my decision to "let go" and count the abundant blessings that I did have. I also had to cleanse and forgive myself every day for the feelings of guilt, sadness, fear and anger that accompanied the losses I had just experienced.

I share my story here with the intention to bring a perspective on the complete process of healing. We all have our stories. We've all been hurt. We've all lost and gained in our lives. We all have perceptions created out of a past. Dissolving our preconceived perceptions every day keeps us in the present moment, so we can be open to receive without the entanglement of negative thoughts. Having gone to the depths of suffering we can rise like the Phoenix, seeing the world through different eyes. I am so very grateful for the "spiritual survival tools" that have brought me full circle to the present time.

In the present moment I have found the soul beyond the soul scars. I found my physical health and emotional healing. I found the magic and the miracle. And I found my friggin' joy. And ... if you are willing, I would like to share it with you.

SECTION 2 – THE PLAQUE OF YOUR SOUL

"The weak can never forgive. Forgiveness is the attribute of the strong."

– Mahatma Gandhi

Chapter 5 – What is the Plaque of Your Soul?

So what is the "plaque of the soul?"

It is a metaphor that just may help us understand what happens to us in life, as we work towards maintaining that innate joy within us. According to Wikipedia, a free online encyclopedia, "plaque" is described as a biofilm, usually colorless, that develops naturally on the teeth. It is formed by colonizing itself to a smooth surface of a tooth. Once it becomes hardened it is difficult to remove. Dental plaque gives rise to tooth decay and the general breakdown of teeth and gums. Plaque builds up if you don't brush your teeth daily. In like manner, our more negative thoughts and emotions build up in our minds and bodies like plaque does to the teeth, and this causes decay, heaviness and depression.

In Section 3 you will learn how to remove the plaque of the soul, the ancient Hawaiian way. The cleansing is more effective when it is done on a daily basis, like when we brush our teeth. Imagine what your teeth would look like if you didn't brush them daily. Likewise, what we ingest from our thoughts – born of a painful or harsh past – weighs heavily on our soul. If we hold onto anything emotionally, that thought-form builds up "plaque" around our unconscious mind, and this in turn affects our physical body. It will affect our body with the blueprint that has been created in our mind. So this form of plaque can build up around the heart when you continually get angry and do not deal with the anger.

We are encouraged from an early age to look outside ourselves for answers. The focus is often on the outer world because that is what we see advertised. If we see and hear anything long enough, the message – whether negative or positive – begins to hypnotize us into accepting its validity. Such a "blueprinting" premise is behind a majority of advertising. Repetition is the mother of skill. It takes 21 days for the unconscious mind to establish a habit. I recently heard an excellent example of this technique with a TV commercial. The advertiser was "whispering" the facts of the product into the ear of the customer. What an excellent ploy! I had to get out of the room and turn it off because the message, and its whispering tactic, was so strong. Our little unconscious mind is quite young and responds well to whispers and baby talk. It does not always respond to the regular conscious mind's voice.

If we get sick, we are told by advertisers to "ask your doctor" who then gives us a prescription or a shot. I'm not recommending you ignore a doctor's advice. I'm simply opposed to the psyche of our society to always be encouraged to look outside ourselves for the answer rather than towards the innate intelligence of the human body to heal itself. We're also told we have to get good grades in school so we can get a college degree. Only then can we expect to get a good job in the market place. Not true anymore. Students leave college to find there are no jobs available. Because of this, they have begun to create jobs of their own. Those who have been laid off have started their own businesses and may be much happier as a result because they are their own boss. The old belief that we'll only be fulfilled if we get married, buy a house and have children is not shared by the majority anymore. In a survey by the National Endowment for Financial Education, nearly half adults surveyed said their top goal was having retirement income, whereas only 17 percent indicated home ownership as a priority. The breakdown of this "American Dream" is happening right before our eyes with the real estate market and economy taking a plunge.

So what am I saying with all of this? It's time we see that all the programming of the collective unconscious need not be our reality. A belief is only held together by the collective that participates in the belief. Gradually our society is taking on a new paradigm based on what each individual really wants in alignment with his or her soul. Imagine what would happen if you stopped believing in your fears? What a concept! I used to be afraid of water, yet for the past 15 years I've been leading groups and individual clients to swim with the wild spinner dolphins in Hawaii. My once paralyzing fear of the water transformed into a feeling of total nurturing by the warm ocean water. Imagine what your life would look like when your walls come tumbling down, when the fear turns to bliss.

You will be living from a deep sense of purpose, in connection with your soul. Now, I do not claim to be an expert on the soul. Yet we all intuitively know when we are in the company of a "good soul" or an "old soul." Then there's Ole King Cole, who was "a merry ole soul, and a merry ole soul was he." We listen to music that "feeds our soul." There is no denying that we feel marvelously uplifted in the presence of spiritual leaders who inspire us to become more enlightened and compassionate. I speak here of the likes of the Dalai Lama and Mother Theresa. Conversely, when we read about despicable acts done by a human being, we cannot help but describe that person's soul as of a "darker nature." I'm referring to someone who has committed unspeakable acts against another without remorse. Those who have committed such crimes have been described in literature and history as having a "dark soul."

How do you explain the difference in these "souls?" Could it be that our souls come through many incarnations learning important lessons about love and compassion? The more "advanced souls" have risen to the wholeness of their spirit and become "teachers" on the planet. We observe the "young souls" still struggling to find meaning in their lives. My first visual experience seeing "a real soul" was at my mother's deathbed. She was 95. I was by her side in the hospital room and heard her take her final breath. I wouldn't allow any hospital staff to take her body away until I could chant some Hawaiian prayers. I was reminded of a film I saw based on the *Tibetan Book of the Dead*. A young man prayed for his dead father at the foot of his bed. As soon as a trickle of blood left one of the father's toes, the son took his father's lifeless body up to a hill to feed the birds of prey. According to Tibetian belief, there was no more emotion because the essence of what was once his father had transitioned.

After about an hour of chanting next to my mother, I saw a puff of grayish white vapor leave her neck and float upward to the shelf above her bed. It paused a moment and then was gone. Was that the soul of my mother leaving her body? I do not know. But the experience certainly left me in a state of peace. It was easier for me to release my mother's body after that experience. It had been raining and stormy all day. Looking out the window at that moment, the clouds lifted and the sunlight poured into my mother's room shinning on her face.

This connection to my mother's soul, which reflected the connection to my own, helped bring me that peace of mind. And it's this peace that I claim for you, so that you may have the full experience of joy you so deserve. By practicing the techniques in this book, you will be able to clean the plaque of your soul and get to that joy.

So how does the plaque accumulate in our bodies in the first place? Again I refer to the ancient Hawaiian teachings of Huna, which Max Freedom Long investigated. Beginning in 1917 and for the next 40 years, he studied with the Kahunas in Hawaii. These spiritual sages were called "Keepers of the Secret." Their magical healings, which were not documented, were disregarded by anthropologists and the missionaries. But Max Freedom Long continued to document what he saw in Hawaii with such books as *The Secret Science at Work* and *Growing Into Light*, showing us how we accumulate the plaque and the negative way of being, as well as the way we can free ourselves of the same. It all starts, in turns out, in the "unconscious mind."

CHAPTER 6 – THE UNCONSCIOUS MIND AND CONSCIOUS MIND

Think of the unconscious mind like the roots of a tree, which sends nutrients to the trunk and the branches. It does so naturally and without any other necessary messages from the tree. Likewise, our unconscious mind feeds us its messages without editing, judgment or any other necessary input. We know our heart is beating at a certain rate, yet we are not telling it to beat. It does this on its own. We don't tell the unconscious mind how to work this inner human operation. It just knows how. Our conscious mind has nothing to do with running the mechanism.

Yet the conscious mind does have an important part to play in our world. It has to be the gatekeeper controlling the emotions of the unconscious so the emotions do not get out of hand. The unconscious – like a little child – does what it wants according to its unbridled will. Like a child, it could eat all the cookies in the cookie jar when left alone. And it might run out in the middle of the street chasing a butterfly, unless the conscious mind, like a caring adult, brings it back. The conscious mind has the important task of creating a balance, as would a responsible parent. You will learn in later chapters how to guide the unconscious with tools you can consciously apply. Learning how to work with the unconscious or "lower self" offers us the key to harmoniously be happy and joyous in our world.

Studying hypnosis in the 1990s, I became fascinated with the function of the unconscious mind and the role that mental suggestions play in healing the body. But I wanted more. Going to Hawaii for my advanced training in Hypnosis and NLP opened the door for me to be introduced to Huna. These ancient teachings revealed even deeper mysteries of the unconscious – that aspect of ourselves which holds the key to connecting with our Higher Self.

According to the Hawaiian Huna teachings, the unconscious is called "Unihipili" or grasshopper. Because our emotions are associated with the element water, the Egyptians gave the grasshopper the symbol of the unconscious mind because a watery substance comes out of a grasshopper's mouth when it is touched. Humans are made up of 80 percent water. Water is a symbol for "mana," or Life Force.

Other names for the unconscious mind in Hawaiian refer to the "child," "low self" or "George." The unconscious acts much like a 2 year old child. It needs repetition to learn a habit. It also cannot be forced into changing a habit. How effective would it be to force a 2 year old to go to bed when he protested? But if you gently read him a soothing bedtime story that he loves, chances are he'll be sound asleep in no time. Likewise, the unconscious must be spoken to in a gentle way – even with a different voice so it knows that you're talking just to "George" – or whatever special name you pick for your unconscious. Even though the unconscious has the will of a 2 year old, its job is to store all our thought-forms that have been created, accepted and accumulated since the beginning of our Creation – from the time we separated from our Divinity. That's a huge task for a 2 year old. These thought-forms – when holding the negative vibrations – are the cause of our problems within our relationships, families, health, environment and society.

These problems are our own responsibility. The causes are within us. Only by dissolving the cause can changes be made. The unconscious knows how to run your body with the present blueprint of unresolved emotions. But it also has a blueprint of perfect health that comes from your Higher Self. We will learn more about accessing this in a later chapter.

Once the unconscious mind has permission from our conscious mind to open up the container of thought-forms, it will do so like an obedient child. No one can interfere with your "free will." So you must consciously WANT to engage the unconscious in your healing.

The conscious and the unconscious work as a TEAM. Think of the unconscious as a faithful computer taking instruction from the conscious mind. Whatever the conscious mind feels or says with emotion (anger, hurt, sadness, guilt, shame), the unconscious will reflect it as it releases a chemical that follows the emotional direction. For example, anger releases a chemical that bruises the heart muscle. What if someone's anger has built up all their life and they never resolved it? It's curious that the leading cause of death in this country, especially among women, is heart attacks. And it's not just from the fatty foods we eat. Constant anger tears at the heart muscle.

The computer does exactly what it's told. For example, Bob hates his job and eventually his unconscious creates an illness so Bob doesn't have to go to work. The emotions of hate and fear weakened Bob's immune system producing an illness. Unconscious motives are primary causes for many destructive events. I had a client we'll call "Jeff" who ended up in a wheelchair as a quadriplegic – the result of being hit by a truck. He admitted to me he was responsible for that accident, as he remembered a destructive thought he was holding at the exact time of the accident. He called me because he was finally ready for the thought-form to leave his mind and body. (De-possession will be discussed in a later chapter.)

More often than not, we know deep down how we create our life situations. We are not victims of our circumstances. When I realized that my "inner dialogue" for years had been "I can't support myself" – reflecting a belief that I needed someone else to support me – my spine or "support system" mirrored that exactly and collapsed. When once we uncover our own unconscious dialogue, then we can consciously change the direction of that inner instruction and thus reverse the symptoms.

Of course, we also have to clear the thought-forms around that subject located in the body. My spine eventually healed after I cleared out my negative thought-forms related to "support" and changed my dialogue to "thank you for supporting me" and "thank you for remembering how to be flexible." I'll discuss in more detail how my spine healed in a later chapter.

The unconscious also does not know how to process a negative. In other words, you can tell a child, "Don't spill the milk," and guess what? You got that right; there goes the milk on the floor. It's almost like a command. It's because **the unconscious does not hear the negative**. "Spill the milk" is impressed upon the mind whether you say to do it or don't do it. I heard a story about a couple climbing a mountain together. They both had their rope lifelines. The woman got to the top first but her husband slipped and was stuck on a ledge. He yelled to her, "Don't let go of the rope." He said it again. "Don't let go of the rope." All she heard was "Let go of the rope." We can guess what happened next. A better exclamation would have been "Pull me up."

Knowing how the unconscious mind learns, we can see how our country has failed in some of its campaigns. "Don't drink and drive." "Don't do drugs." Don't, don't, don't. Right now, I would like for you to not think of a blue kangaroo. You have to think about that which you don't want to think about before you don't think about it. So now you know how it works. Impressions upon the mind will help manifest that impression in the physical world.

So how can we reach the unconscious mind? One way is the pendulum. This is a semi-heavy stone attached to a string or chain, which is dangled by the thumb and first finger. A key chain can also be used. With the pendulum, you can only ask the unconscious yes or no questions. You wouldn't ask open-ended questions or random questions about winning lottery numbers. It doesn't pick numbers. It knows a yes and a no. Establish first what the direction for "yes" is. While dangling the stone, watch the direction it moves. If it moves up and down then that is your "yes." Then ask it to give you a "big yes." If it moves in a clockwise circle then that's your "big yes." Do the same for the direction of "no." This technique works very well for shopping or even buying new vitamins. Say you are undecided about what brand to take. Hold each bottle in your hand and ask the pendulum "Is this something that will enhance my body and be for my highest good?" If the pendulum swings in the "no" direction then walk away. Your unconscious mind knows the truth of what it needs to be healthy. Working much like muscle testing, this technique is helpful since you can do it yourself.

We must use tools such as pendulums since we are as yet not completely in communion with the unconscious mind and the Higher Self. If we could all remember how to be as innocent as we were from ages 1 - 7, we'd know how the unconscious mind works. This is why it's so much fun to be around children. I play with my 6-year-old grandson at the park twice a week. I'm so grateful for this. I watch him come down the slide backwards or frontwards, spinning like a gyroplane on a swing or just running through the grass after the squirrels. He displays his pure unconscious mind living in the moment with no thought of past or future. It is only after the age of seven that the critical conscious mind develops and the consequences of life begin to set in. Some people grow up and forget the wonder of being "childlike." They become rigid in their thoughts and allow the mere conscious mind to run their world. They move away from the purity of the unconscious, which holds the key to the healing of your body. If we listen to the unconscious mind it will always tell us the truth. This is our gut feeling – the "red flags" to which we're supposed to pay attention. Successful people in all walks of life listen to their instincts or unconscious mind and they have not forgotten how to be playful. It is also the key to staying young at heart.

The ego – which is attached to the conscious mind – literally wants to kill you. This is because the ego is all about the physical body. It will tell you to look for love everywhere outside yourself. Go to that seminar, buy that dress, if you were thinner, if you were prettier, if you were younger and on and on. The ego is relentless telling you that "you're not enough the way you are." But it's all a LIE. The ego creates fear and false stories to keep its investment alive.

Author Carolyn Myss created an analogy for the Higher Self, which may aid in our understanding. She refers to the Higher Self as the symbol of Snow White, from Disney fame. She says Snow White represents the Higher Self, while the dwarfs represent the seven chakras, which she tries to clean before letting them come back to the cottage. The Wicked Witch stands for the ego trying to kill Snow White just as the ego wants to prevent us from knowing our Higher Self. I find it curiously synchronistic that I applied to be a Tour Guide at Disneyland in the 60's but was cast as the character Snow White instead.

If you believe the stories and dissolutions of the ego, you will lose your self-esteem and may develop a destructive habit, like drugs, to quiet the negative thoughts. Drugs and alcohol feed the ego as does caffeine, nicotine and sugar. When you eliminate these substances you QUIET THE EGO and then can listen to the TRUTH coming from the UNCONSCIOUS MIND. I recently heard an interview with the businessman, Donald Trump. Whether you like him or not, it was interesting that he admitted that he didn't smoke, drink or do drugs of any kind in his life. He chose that lifestyle because his elder brother had been an alcoholic. As a result, his mind was clearer to trust his intuition.

In basic terms, refraining from destructive habits, quieting the ego's attempt to distract, and following the intuitive messages that come from our gut, or "George," or unconscious mind, helps us on the path of peace and that wonderful inner joy.

Chapter 7 – The Trouble That has been Accumulating

I have heard it said, "There is no stress in the world, only people with stressful thoughts." Think about what that means. Stress is only created by the person thinking the thought.

I was with a young friend today who was completely broken up because her boyfriend does not pay attention to her needs. For starters, he did not do anything for her on Valentine's Day. When she asks him a question, he puts on earphones, rather than answer her, and he continues to disrespect her. You might wonder why she stays with such a person. There are good times in this relationship, but lately all I hear is the abuse. Nothing changes. The tears keep flowing. When I suggest she could look at him in a different way, she defends him and her story. Her emotions are so strongly attached to the drama of her story that she doesn't want to look at it differently. What she doesn't know is the stress of this situation only takes place in her mind. If we know that our minds can make up a story (that's what the conscious mind does), then we can make up a productive story rather than a destructive one. If we do not have the ability to change our stories, then the accumulation of stress on our bodies piles up and eventually causes illness. My young friend wears her heart on her sleeve. Hopefully, in her maturing, she will soon open her eyes and make different choices.

In this section of the book, I intend to show that we have been accumulating our own troubles, our own upset, and our own plaque over time. And such trouble is something that we can transform when we realize we are the ones holding onto it.

Imagine a string of pearls. From the beginning of the clasp there is a first pearl that starts the whole strand. Imagine that first pearl containing the deepest wound you carry, for example, unworthiness. If "unworthiness" begins the strand, then you are likely to attract similar "pearls" or events that match up with the first strand, thus proving "unworthiness" as a reality you believe you must accept. You might even say to yourself, "See, I knew it was too good to be true." Money slips through your hands, relationships end before they even begin, all because of a deep unconscious belief that you are unworthy to receive.

My young friend in a relationship may have the unworthiness wound because she has attracted a painful relationship. If she reverses her belief about herself at the deepest level, then perhaps her boyfriend will look at her differently and treat her with more kindness. She must transform her vibration on the inside before a boyfriend will respond differently to her.

When you feel like a victim, you invite another person to take advantage of you. Predators seek out victims. Owning your own power stops the cycle. Consciously believing that you are "truly worthy to receive" brings abundance in all forms. The ocean never runs out of water. The waves constantly come in and move out. So abundant blessings flow from the always abundant ocean, and we simply have to be ready to feel the worthiness. This is a spiritual law of the natural order of things. If you think you do not deserve to receive, then the Universe will not appear to offer you the gift. It goes to someone who believes they do deserve to receive. Our thoughts either bring in the gifts or block them. If we see the world as struggling for survival, then we must change the way we're looking at ourselves.

I have an older friend who recently lost his wife of 30 years. Losing your life partner is huge, and many times the one left behind does not fare well alone. But Henry is an optimist. He loves being social and is always present with a smile. He told me he felt lonely and had a difficult time going home to an empty house. Then he decided that his home could become his "sanctuary" instead of a sad place. As soon as he changed the "meaning" of being alone in his mind, his attitude changed as well. Henry turned a "stressful situation" around and created something beneficial – probably even adding many more years to his life.

What negative thoughts do you say to yourself that could be changed in a positive way? If you say you are depressed you will continue to be. What about being "temporarily down?" This even applies to being tired or broke. I remember hearing Michael Todd, one of Elizabeth Taylor's husbands, say when he lost his money, "I'm only temporarily broke." He later made back his fortune. When I was preparing for a Formula Ford race I started to get a panicky feeling because I was feeling really scared with all the track noise. I decided to convince myself that I was "excited" to be experiencing this event. The emotions of excitement and fear transpire in the same pit of the stomach. My conscious mind helped make sure I felt excitement rather than fear, and this got me more prepared to race. Actually, the acronym "FEAR" can mean Feeling Excited And Ready. It can also mean False Evidence Appearing Real. Whichever way you look at it, your conscious mind has the power to guide your thoughts and emotions.

Remember, the purpose of this book is for you to find your friggin' joy despite what life throws at you. You are able to interpret the "meaning" of what happens in your life in order to accelerate your highest good. "To choose one's attitude in any given circumstance is to choose one's own way," said Viktor Frankl, renowned survivor of the Auschwitz concentration camp. The Nazi guards could not control his attitude and spiritual well-being. Viktor found his strength to stay alive by thinking about his loving wife. He found a meaning to life even when faced with a hopeless situation.

Sometimes joy is challenging to access when we hang on to that which doesn't serve us. There are people who feel the woes of the world more than others and have a harder time letting go of attachments to outcomes. Attachment is the number one cause of suffering. If you cannot detach from the outcome, you are sure to suffer when things don't turn out as you wish. Herein lays the meaning of the saying, "Go with the flow."

In considering this concept, I'm often drawn back to my experience in the ocean when I was first learning to swim in Hawaii after a lifetime water phobia. Feeling confident one day, I found myself further out than I had anticipated and got caught in a swirling undercurrent. Not knowing what to do in this situation, I started to panic, and this resulted in staying right where I was and using a lot of energy to get nowhere. Running out of steam, I called out for help but there was no one around. Suddenly out of nowhere, emerged a giant turtle at my side. Looking into the turtle's eyes, I sensed him say, "Do what I do." Immediately I stopped struggling and my arms began to move up and down with the turtle's slow and deliberate movements. We locked eyes and floated together. The turtle guided me over the current and placed me gently on the rocks. By the time I caught my breath and looked around for him…he had disappeared. I owe my life to the turtle and have never forgotten the lesson. When you are caught in the current, adjust, and go with what is happening. Holding on too tightly will have you struggle with that which you are holding. Only the "letting go" of the struggle gives us a chance to return to a higher way of being. This is absolutely the same premise found in the ancient Hawaiian forgiveness process we'll discuss in Section 3. Just as I stopped struggling with the ocean current, we are invited to release our perceptions of what binds us. By doing so, we give ourselves the chance to reconnect with our desires at a higher level.

My belief is that as you become a more advanced soul, you will not be able to hang on to the past. Only present time will be of importance. If you are invested in the world's problems, then the media will make sure you never forget bad or tragic events. The events are repeated ad nauseam every hour on the hour so the general public never forgets. Remember 9/11? We will never forget that horrific event because the visions of the planes crashing into the twin towers have been repeatedly etched into our memory. Remember that the unconscious mind only needs 21 repetitions before it establishes a habit. When you feel emotionally invested in any event it sticks to your emotional unconscious body and will be triggered whenever you experience anything resembling the event. If this happens often to you, you'll be dragged down energetically because of the energetic weight building up inside.

I was in my tax accountant's office the other day and noticed a bottle of "Goo Gone" on his desk. Oh, it would be so awesome if we could clean all the "goo" inside of us with a little "Goo Gone." Well, you will be able to do just that by transforming your perception of past events, thereby making the environment inside of you more neutral. The result of cleaning up this field will lighten you up, keeping you in the present time.

Chapter 8 – How do we Store Emotions?

Emotions are stored at the unconscious level when we experience an emotional event. For example, if you're in a car accident and hear a song on the radio at the time of impact, you will always feel scared or jumpy when that song is played again. In other words, that song becomes your "button pusher" for that emotion. Some people resent being hugged. In this situation, those people were somehow hugged at a time that was either uncomfortable or emotional for them, perhaps being hugged at the funeral of a loved one. The unconscious registers the event with the emotion when it is in a highly charged state. I'm sure you remember smells from your childhood, or sentimental movies, or familiar places. All things that bring up emotion are stored by "George," our unconscious mind. We all can name a friend or a family member who let their emotions rule them. Their lives are like emotional roller coasters. They fly off the handle at any little trigger. When we become "conscious" then we must understand how to control our emotional body. How long would you want to wallow in the sadness or the hurt?

Relationships are constantly testing our emotional buttons. And if you really want to move to a higher level emotionally, you can start by accepting that it's never about the other person. It's always about you. I was seeing someone whom I thought would make a great partner in a mature loving relationship. He seemed different from the others because he actually had a good reputation for healing people. The first red flag was hearing about his relationship with his mother. My first rule – a guy treats you exactly as he treats his mother, with very few exceptions. So if he doesn't speak highly of his mother, you should look elsewhere. Obviously, I didn't follow my rule. Hearing him rant about wanting nothing to do with his mother should have sent me packing. Instead I waited to see if maybe he would be the exception to the rule. We laughed a lot, had great conversations, enjoyed hikes and movies, and the chemistry was great. We were even taking things slowly which I've never been known to do. But he would disappear for weeks at a time with hardly a phone call. Then Valentine's Day came and went, and still no word from him. Needless to say, I was hurt and saddened by his behavior. I wallowed in some self-pity for a few days and then consciously dissolved my perception of what happened and how I was feeling. I knew he wouldn't change. We can't change anyone. We can only change our own nature and the way we're looking at a situation. I felt I was ready to move on after doing some conscious "cord cutting" (explained in Chapter 14 – Ho'oponopono). I decided I deserved to bring in a man who honors and truly loves a woman, having shared such respect with his own mother.

This topic reminds me of a beautiful poem by Lisa Citore: *If You Want to Change the World ... Love a Woman - Just One Woman* (from *Magdalene Women*). She wrote:

> "If you want to change the world ... love a woman - really love her. Love her for life-beyond your fear of death, beyond your fear of being manipulated by the Mother inside your head. If you want to change the world ... love a woman to the depths of your shadow, to the highest reaches of your Being, back to the Garden where you first met her, to the gateway of the rainbow realm where you walk through together as Light as One, to the point of no return, to the ends and the beginning of a new Earth."

My male friend claimed he wanted to change the world through his shamanic practices. He would collect road kill and dead bones for his sacred journeys, selflessly bring gifts to the Native American Indians, spending more time investing in the past rather than living in the present from the heart. I was angry with him at first. But after doing the "cord cutting" our paths crossed again, and my heart melted into compassion for him. Now I could see him through different eyes. We verbally communicated and were able to resolve the illusions we had of one another, thus reaching a deeper level of understanding. Had I not done the cord cutting ritual I might have missed the opportunity to grow with this person. He pushed my buttons so I could go deeper within and make the changes inside myself. It's always all about us taking the responsibility. If you want to clean the plaque of your soul, then you must take responsibility to cleanse yourself so you can look out of your eyes and see a brighter picture.

When someone chooses the past over the present (doesn't cleanse the plaque), there is a heavy burden laid upon the heart. Wouldn't it feel better to resolve the negative emotions of the past so that we can live joyfully in the present? Taking the burden off our heart is the journey of a lifetime. But we can start consciously, as we now have simple ways to get a head start. The only requirement is that we are ready to make the changes on the inside. How committed are you to leave this planet with a soul upgrade? How important is it for you to "lighten your load" and find your friggin' joy? The ancient Egyptians believed that when people died, in order for their soul to reach the next highest level; their heart had to be lighter than the feather of truth. The heart of the deceased was actually weighed on a scale. If the heart was lighter than the feather it could pass on. But if it were heavier, it would be devoured by the demon Ammut. How much does your heart weigh if your life were to end right now? We all have some conscious work to do. Let's make the most of it.

CHAPTER 9 – THE BUTTON PUSHERS

What would you say if you knew the people who "push your buttons" were your soul mates? I kid you not. I remember hearing Wayne Dyer say this at one of his lectures years ago. I had a hard time wrapping my mind around that pearl of wisdom. We all expect our soul mate to be someone who warms the embers of our heart. At best, he or she would finish our sentences, love the same movies and share the same passions. But to really cleanse ourselves on the inside, we have to find out what's eating us. If we stay hiding out in a cave all our lives – which some people do – we'll never have our buttons pushed. It takes being in a relationship with another human being to really push our buttons. If we want to be conscious, then we are invited to understand why we get irritated when we get our buttons pushed. Button pushers remind us of the wounds we're still concealing deep inside. You know you have a physical problem when you experience pain in your body. You push the spot and yell in discomfort. When a friend or loved one doesn't compliment the dinner you worked so hard to make, or makes a rude comment about your wardrobe choice, you either let it roll off your back or you become irritated. If you become irritated you know your button has been pushed. No one likes to be insulted. But this time you are especially annoyed because, say, it brings up how you felt as a child growing up with a critical father.

And sometimes the triggers go even deeper. For example, I never knew my father. He left when I was a year and a half, and my name was changed to negate all remnants of my half-Irish ancestry. The men I've attracted, including my ex-husband, have not been emotionally available and never quite measured up to the imaginary bar I've set so high. When I let someone in, they either run back into their cave or disappear entirely. My most recent relationship certainly allowed me to see deeper into the pattern I was creating. But this time we're both hanging in there and enjoying the ride. One of us had to be willing to see something differently. Since I'm writing this book, I have to put myself on the line and show how it works. Talk is cheap. The proof is always in the pudding.

Some of the inner shadows we must face appear around the all-too-familiar button pusher of money. You can compare our energy to our finances. Think about our energy as money, wherein we're only given about $100 a day in energy. Ideally, we are to save as much energy as we can because we might use it later when our body is challenged with a severe illness. Many people, not being conscious of how they spend their energy, waste a lot of their money. Think about it. Anger is an acceptable emotion in our culture. Just watch a football game or a tennis match where an umpire or referee gives a "questionable call." The players lose their cool and the crowd goes wild. No one gives a thought to the effects of this anger on their hearts. Let's say someone cuts you off as you drive to work in the morning. You get very angry in the car and by the time you get to work you are already exhausted because you have already spent $80 of your energy. By the end of the day you are in deficit. By the time you get home, all you can do is lie down on the couch because you're too tired to do anything. Giving in to our emotions may energetically bankrupt us.

It takes energy to take action on new ideas. We need all the Life Force and energy we can muster to take our creative ideas out into the marketplace. The next time someone cuts in front of you on the way to work, you might consider being "a teensy bit annoyed" and spending only $10 of your energy. With such choices, now you're being fully conscious. You'll be amazed at how good you'll feel, because you won't be spending the energy to hold down the emotions of the past. When the stuff of the past begins to roll off your back, you are truly beginning to live from the present instead of reacting to the past.

I have another example of becoming conscious of our past emotions and the weight it has on our heart. I was watching an Oprah show. On this particular show, Oprah was reunited with a half-sister she never knew existed. This half-sister tried for years to get in touch with Oprah but never went to the tabloids. Years before, Oprah's other sister, went to the tabloids to expose Oprah's failed pregnancy when she was 14 years old. Oprah revealed how angry and betrayed she felt when this sister sold the story to the tabloids for $20,000. Now this new half-sister, who shared the same mother as Oprah, never went to the tabloids. Oprah found out through the family that her mother had another baby and gave her up for adoption because she didn't want to be on welfare any longer. Oprah realized that the "shame" her mother still felt kept her mother stuck inside, resulting in illness. Oprah had another major realization. She admitted that the sister who "betrayed her" had really done her a favor by telling the tabloids about her secret pregnancy. She realized the benefit of releasing negative emotions from the past, and instead of carrying a dark and painful secret, Oprah did not have to carry that burden on her heart any longer. She was free of the weight of that secret.

Chapter 10 – Explaining
the Unexplainable

As a civilization we're moving forward faster than ever before. If you don't prepare yourself on the inside, you will likely be caught up in a whirlpool of fear and unresolved emotion. The news is filled with disasters in our outer world: earthquakes, floods, military uprisings, government breakdowns, corporations crumbling, real estate devaluation, oil spills, gas prices, water shortages and on and on. We are tenants temporarily living on Mother Earth. She will right the wrongs done to Her over time. How you handle what is happening in the world will reveal how SECURE you feel inside yourself. It is said that we are living in the DREAM we have made by our COLLECTIVE THOUGHTS. When we stop believing in the dream it will change its structure. When people stopped believing in Communism in East Berlin, the Berlin Wall fell. The majority of people now seem to be freeing themselves from conventional ideas that don't work any longer. If it doesn't feel good at the truth level, you need not participate. No one wants to be ruled by a dictator, and now the people are standing up and saying "no more." As things change in our outside world, we begin to see how it is possible to change our inner world, especially if our ideas are somewhat outdated.

For example, take the way we've been conditioned to think about healing. The general consensus tells us to go to a doctor when we have an illness. But I'll bet when you were young, the majority of you had your "boo-boo's" kissed away by a well-meaning adult. We knew the boo-boo would heal by itself in just a few days. How many of us will know with conviction that we will be fine again when illness strikes?

As we grow older and develop more conscious skepticism, we lose touch with our connection to our UNCONSCIOUS MIND ... the part of us that RUNS OUR BODY. We already talked about how our unconscious mind serves as the computer to our conscious mind's commands. So if you really want to communicate with the unconscious and change the negative patterns you've been accumulating, then begin to listen to what you're saying to yourself. Are these things you would want anyone to hear? What's your inner script? When you are aware enough to be able to write those phrases down, you'll see what direction your unconscious mind is taking and why your body has been doing what it's been doing.

Eric, 58, in a wheelchair, came to me for a healing session. At 19 he broke his neck in a car accident. He told me he knew he had set up this accident long before it happened. Unconsciously, he wanted to know what it felt like to be paralyzed. Whatever the unconscious believes to be true becomes your reality. Now Eric was ready to heal himself from feeling like a victim. He has been able to unplug from the burden of "victim thinking" thus freeing himself to be lighter. Now, he invited his Higher Self to begin the healing.

Martha had cancer when she came to see me years ago. At the time I was doing only hypnosis and past-life regression. At five years of age, Martha's mother died suddenly. As a child unable to understand death, Martha decided that she was to blame for her mother's death. Developing cancer was her way of punishing herself and ultimately joining her mother. In the regression, Martha's mother revealed herself and the reason for her death, which had nothing to do with Martha. Finally getting the closure she needed, Martha's body began to respond to the medication given to her to stop the cancer. Martha recovered from the cancer. Our unconscious desires are running our body. Getting in touch with the way they have been programmed will open our eyes to how we want to proceed. The unconscious also holds the key to reach the Higher Self, which ultimately knows how to heal our illness.

As a Huna Practitioner of ancient Hawaiian healing, I learned about the three Selves of Man and the role the Higher Self (which is in all of us) plays to change our DNA and heal the physical body. For the ancient Hawaiians, the ultimate goal was to reach the Higher Self. Clearing the unconscious mind of the negative thought-forms from the past, you can then send your "desires" up the pipeline to the Higher Self for activation.

I experienced this myself 16 years ago, when my spine collapsed with nerve damage. My son Brian was living with me in Tiburon and carried me to bed when I could no longer walk. I was told by medical doctors that I wouldn't walk again without surgery. Brian and another well-meaning friend urged me to go the "safer surgical route." Not wanting to be cut, I decided to put the Huna recipe into action. Within four days of actively doing these processes, my back recovered completely ... even healing my scoliosis I had since birth. Shocked that I could walk again and feel normal, Brian was more fearful of his own "inner cleansing process" which he was not ready to comprehend. Personally, it felt like I had won the lottery, only better. I could heal myself together with my Higher Self. These Huna practices really worked! That brought me lots of friggin' joy! I decided to devote my life to teaching others how they could do the same.

So how do you explain the unexplainable? How do you explain calculus to a 3-year-old? Reaching our Higher Self is what some of us aspire to in hopes of receiving Divine Truth, yet it can belong to the realm of the unfathomable, to our limited conscious mind. Healing my back was nothing short of a miracle to me. Yet, the recipe was available and I followed it, as I clearly believed in it.

And now, if you are ready, if you make the choice to believe, we have for you the cleansing and the ancient cleaning practices and techniques that can bring back to you – if you are willing – your friggin' joy.

SECTION 3 – THE CLEANSING OF YOUR SOUL

"To forgive is to set a prisoner free and discover that the prisoner was you."

- Lewis B. Smedes

Chapter 11 – The Great Secret Teachings: Missing Links Revealed

Recently I found myself in a conversation with three gentlemen. Almost immediately I sensed a tension in the elder gentleman and told him I was writing a book about cleansing your soul in order to find your joy. He revealed he had too many regrets about his past to feel he could ever find any joy. Most of his life he had been a judge in a military tribunal, and some of the past events were coming back to haunt him. He believed it was too much to overcome. When I told him the book would give him ways to connect with his Higher Self, which would assist him in forgiving himself of his past, he was interested in reading the book. You don't have to be stuck in the past. There is an easy way to be in the present and to be joyful. It's found in the ancient Huna teachings born in the beauty of Hawaii.

When I was first introduced to Huna almost 20 years ago, I was intrigued by its definition: "leading a hurt-less life." What did that mean? Well, I came to understand it as one refraining from doing or saying anything to harm yourself or another. The word "Huna" – devised by the teacher and author Max Freedom Long to mean "secret" – is the name of the teachings of the ancient Hawaiian people.

Over thousands of years old, the teachings are comprised of the original teachings of the people of this Earth. Before 750 C.E. (Common Era) all the people of the Earth lived by the Huna teachings of a connection with the Higher Self and a balanced male and female energy system. At that time, people recognized that the real "power" came from the One

Source called the "I'O." This knowledge was taught all over the planet in a way best understood by the native peoples. In approximately 325 C.E., a wave of male-dominate cultures presided over the planet and overthrew the balanced systems. The sacred original teachings were wiped out, such as those from the Native Americans and the Australian Aboriginals. As time progressed, people deviated from the early teachings, separating themselves from Spirit and creating new beliefs and doctrines. Over the years, Huna remained pure because the Hawaiian Islands were distant from other cultures. Fortunately, the wise teachers sent many of the sacred teachings underground, knowing the cycle would eventually shift back towards balance. Because of this, the teachings remained a secret and were considered to be the most direct link to the ancient wisdom. In Hawaii, the original teachings were hidden in chants and Hula dances. By 1820, the Christian missionaries began to eliminate the old "superstitious ways." They considered these teachings to be "sorcery" and "witchcraft."

Anyone who was caught practicing these rituals was fined and imprisoned. This was the case especially for the Kahunas, the master healers of the order. Though misguided, the missionaries were simply living by their own dogma and control without any awareness of a Higher Consciousness. Before the missionaries came, the Hawaiians lived their lives relatively free of mental illness. They were aligned with the Great Spirit through their breathing and forgiveness practices. When they noticed that the missionaries were not fully breathing, and yet "telling" them about God, the Hawaiians knew the missionaries couldn't send strong enough prayers to reach the God force. Consequently, the Hawaiians did not reveal their secrets.

The sacred word "I'O" which referred to the Highest Creation (Akasha/Void) was given the designation of "hawk" (one who flies to the higher limits) because they did not want their sacred word desecrated by the missionaries' lack of consciousness. The word for the missionaries became "haole" which meant "without breath." The non-native people in Hawaii are still regarded as "haoles" today by Hawaiians because of their shallow breathing.

It was considered illegal to teach Huna practices in Hawaii from 1820 to the late 1970's. The United States Government passed the Native

American Religious Freedoms Act in 1979, which has allowed these ancient healing techniques to be practiced once more. Over the past 30 years, our entire planet has experienced a return to the ancient ways of connecting with Spirit and a higher energy. The old male-dominated institutions are presently crumbling primarily because they fail to teach cooperation, they subtly deny the rights of women (the feminine), and they negate Spirit in all its forms. Denying this Divine Connection has only brought us disharmony, dissolution, depression, despair and war.

We have all participated in this collective dream, and now this dream is presently coming to an end. Outdated models, like the dinosaurs, become extinct. As our awareness continues to unfold, we are realizing we are energy beings and that our thoughts have created our reality. All the scriptures tell us that at one time we were one, united "whole." But separation from Spirit arose from the belief that we were separate. The purpose of dominant societies was to create power struggles and separation as well as to keep people's minds controlled and in fear. When the mind is in fear, it is in opposition to the heart, which is total and complete love. Fear blocks the heart from opening and trusting. When you are in fear, you can also be manipulated. We have seen this countless times in our history, with dictators taking over countries, governments waging wars and politicians leveraging their control. As Sir Winston Churchill wisely stated, "Those who fail to learn from history are doomed to repeat it."

And so, knowing about the past wisdom of Huna, knowing the results of a controlled culture, knowing the consequences of fear and separation on our souls and on our society, what shall we do?

In a word "forgive." Yet this endeavor – done quite simply and swiftly by the practitioner of the great secret Huna teachings – has been an arduous if not impossible one for most of us.

So how does this Huna forgiveness technique work, whereas other endeavors to forgive may not? Have you ever tried to simply and swiftly forgive an enemy or foe who may have done you "wrong?" Have you ever tried to pretend everything was "fine" in the face of your resentment over a past experience? Have you ever had a parental figure just say, "Tell him you are sorry" and then do so with a gut full of frustration? Such attempts at forgiveness and release are futile, for they are missing some vital pieces of the puzzle. And what are those missing links? Simply put here, and then revealed in depth for the remainder of this section are such pieces:

1. Being prepared mentally – using your free will to choose a path that will take courage to truly face what you have been avoiding

2. The power of the breath – using the "HA breath" found in the Huna healing process

3. The connection to your Higher Self or a supreme Life Force

4. The vital process of cutting and dissolving cords or negative ties to people and experiences

5. Embracing the stringent reality that this forgiveness is actually about you forgiving yourself for your perceptions – not the life experiences – that have hurt you

6. The continual, committed and routine practice of clearing negative ties, dissolving cords, and cleansing the soul

If one takes these steps, the pathway to freedom and joy will easily be secured. But it will take your choice born of bravery and courage. And so I say, make the decree, make the call! Call back your Spirit! This involves the decision – your choice now – to melt away the anger, fear and resentments that have calcified our hearts. As a nation, we will then be stepping into the higher vibrations of Divine Love and Compassion ... one person at a time. Already we feel the strong vibrations of the planet moving us away from war, greed and the ways of being that no longer serve us. Countries dominated by dictators are falling because the people will not support them. The old dreams are shattering like bubbles bursting in the air. We are gradually beginning to incorporate what does work. New and harmonious ways of living together within the community of Earth provide us with a unity for all, a connection to a Higher Self and respect for all of life.

Chapter 12 – Connecting with the Higher Self

I n W.R Glover's book *Huna, the Ancient Religion of Positive Thinking*, the author compares the three selves of man to a house. There's a basement, a first floor and an attic. Imagine you're sitting in your house looking out of the windows. You can see with your five senses the trees outside, traffic, people walking their dogs and much more. Compare this scenario to the ability of your Conscious Mind to be in tune with the outside world. Yet this level of mind is limited in its ability to see deeper. Now imagine that in your house you have a basement, which you never visit because the door is normally locked. Your unconscious mind lives and works in the basement, but has the power to run your body, based on the present blueprint of past, unresolved memories. You never get to see it unless you invite yourself to clean it out once in a while. Unknown to you, your conscious mind registers all its observations directly to the unconscious in the basement, and it's this level that does exactly as it's told. The conscious mind sends down the facts as presented to the five senses and the unconscious records and files them as "memories."

Now up in the attic lives your Higher Self. The Higher Self gets to see more without the distractions of the physical world. Everyone has a Higher Self, no exceptions, though most people are not in contact with their Higher Self. The Higher Self – akin to our God Self – will not interfere with your free will. It has the power to heal our bodies and create so-called "miracles" in our lives. It holds perfectly balanced male and female energy. The Higher Self receives the transmission of a desire from the unconscious mind much like we consciously put out a prayer request to the Universe. The conscious mind has communication only with the unconscious mind. The unconscious mind, on the other hand, has direct communication with the Higher Self. This is why we must clear the pipeline of thought-forms so our "desires" get taken up to the Higher Self for the sake of creation. According to the teachings, you must go through the unconscious to get to the Higher Self.

This concept of the three selves has even been depicted in Egyptian hieroglyphics (picture writing). These drawings are revealed at the back of Max Freedom Long's book *What Jesus Taught in Secret*. For example, to show the three combined selves of man you will see three storks (the symbol of a spirit-being) fused together to become one.

Connecting to one's Higher Self brings a total connection to all of creation and re-creation. Earlier in the book, I mentioned that 15 years ago I was told I had spinal paralysis and disc degeneration and would not walk again without surgery. Instead of the surgery, I chose to clear out the negative dialogue and thought-forms from my unconscious and create a spine that could easily be flexible and climb trees again. It worked for me! After letting the old memories release through the Huna teachings of "Ho'oponopono," I would get emotionally excited about climbing trees again. That emotion or desired prayer was sent along the invisible pipeline to my Higher Self, which changed the DNA of my body and gave me a new spine. I don't know how the Higher Self did it. And I don't have to know. My job was only to clear out the pipeline and get the unconscious mind to perceive what I wanted to be created, and do so in an emotionally focused manner. In this way – by getting emotionally invested and charged – the unconscious will expedite the order in sending your desires up the pipeline to your Higher Self.

Chapter 13 – Cutting Cords in the "Forgiveness Process"

As I write this in early 2011, I've been carrying great sadness for the people of Japan as a tsunami struck their country resulting in a radioactive meltdown. My beloved Hawaii was also affected 5,000 miles away. Some homes were lifted from their foundation and found floating in the bay. It's hard to fathom this force of Mother Nature being so gentle on one hand and then literally destroying what She created. I could not write during this time as I had been processing what had happened. Finally, I felt that it was time to "cut my cords" of sadness about the event, in order to move forward.

We can't help but get emotional about the events in our lives. On one level we are connected to those dear hearts with whom we feel aligned. On another level, we are connected to all people all over the world. The Internet makes it possible for us to learn instantly when tragedy strikes. So even though we've read there have always been earthquakes, tsunamis, floods, volcanic eruptions and mass upheavals since time began, we get to experience it now as though it's happening to us personally. The more we are emotionally invested in any event, the more we will attach invisible energetic "cords" via our unconscious mind. If your conscious mind keeps allowing these cords to accumulate, as it did for me this week, then heaviness will set in, which is no more than an accumulation of connecting cords.

What would happen if you decided to stop brushing your teeth for a week? I don't have to describe how that might feel in your mouth. Most people would not let that happen because they've been trained to be clean on the outside. So now become aware that without cleaning out the unconscious mind, and without cutting the energetic cords that keep us connected to that which doesn't serve us, we are collecting plaque on our soul. We must find a way to "brush up" and keep that part of us clean and clear. It will assist us in being pure channels of creation and being the bearer of all the friggin' joy you can imagine!

To help you keep clean, I will take you through a step-by-step process to unplug from the way you are presently looking at a person, event or problem, especially if that connection is clogged with negative thoughts or emotions.

NUMBER ONE, know that you cannot change what happened in the past. It happened. But the good news is you can change the way you look at it, as you "unplug" from your common perception of it. At first, as you do this process, you might have an emotional reaction and feel sadness or fear, as I did with the tsunami event in Japan. The mind may continue to make up more stories to support a buildup of emotions. In regards to an unfortunate past event, you have to decide with your own "free will" that it's time to "let it go" and begin again. Know that what you are "letting go" of is only the way you look at the event or person. You have the opportunity to perceive differently and transform a thought-form that drags your energy down into a perception that uplifts and enlivens you. In fact, this is how you can tell you need to "cut cords" – if you feel the fear, anger, sadness, hate, guilt, revenge, that simply drags you down. Replacing these energies with the sweet and light energy of love will help you to move forward in life.

So, the process? It's called "HO'OPONOPONO."

In the original teachings of Ho'oponopono, the Hawaiians of old would gather as a family every night at sunset and do the Ho'oponopono process. Ho'o means "to make;" pono means "right." So by definition, in this process you would make right-right (two times) inside yourself. If you had said anything during the day to hurt yourself or harm another, you would cut the cord that bound you to that event. In the process, all negative thought-forms melt into the water with the sunset, as you offer forgiveness through your Higher Self, which never judged you or anyone for anything in the first place.

According to your Higher Self, you have never done anything wrong, but the ego has made you think you have done something wrong. Forgiveness is done with the permission of the conscious mind, but the actual forgiveness comes from the Higher Self, which ironically sees nothing to forgive ... except perhaps a mistaken perception.

Since we carry past hurts inside us, we are essentially correcting past wrongs with all of our ancestors, relatives, and friends by embracing the concept of Ho'oponopono. Healing these ancient wounds is perhaps the greatest gift we can give our planet and ourselves. If you come from a lineage of angry, fearful, or resentful people, imagine the impact of clearing that past so the old anger or fear does not continue into the next generation. How many times have you had conversations within yourself with your mother or father, a loved one, or the IRS? If there is negative energy around this dialogue, you are forming "cords" around your aura-field that depletes your energy. Hawaiians called these ethereal cords "AKA." Sticky "AKA cords," with an alternating current that flows between two people, accumulate in the body and can have you feeling all tied up at times. You know you have AKA build-up if you would rather pull the covers over your head or sit staring at the TV rather than start a new project, or in my case, finish writing this book. Procrastination is a great way to put off following your dreams, because you lack the motivation or energy to move forward.

Another way you may feel "drained" from AKA cords is when you are with someone who drains your energy. If a person can't access their own energy, they will attempt to suck it from someone who has more to offer. Once you cut the cords from these "energy vampires," you can work with the White Light and "intend" to keep your own aura field strong. Your "internal" electric bill may be too costly if you have plugged into too many emotional sockets. It may be time to lower your internal electric bill, especially if you are healing from a disease, and need all the energy to help heal yourself.

Ho'oponopono is a process that aligns everything inside of us and helps clean up our relationships with people from our past and present, by dissolving or cutting the negative cords of discord. Such dissolutions will reveal the only truth that stands. For the truth is: all there is ... is

LOVE. This is Divine Love as opposed to our own interpretation of what love is based on our past experiences. You will only be "cutting cords" or dissolving your agenda with these people and events. YOU CAN NEVER CUT THE CORD OF DIVINE LOVE. Once you cut the cords with people and events, all that will remain is LOVE in the purest form.

An updated version of the Ho'oponopono process was developed by Morrnah Nalamaku Simeona, who taught this form throughout the United States, Europe and Asia. Morrnah – who passed away February 11, 1992 in Hirchhelm, Germany – was recognized as a kahuna lapa'au (healer) and honored as a "Living Treasure of Hawai'I" by the Honpa Hongwanji Mission of Hawaii.

I had the honor of encountering Morrnah when I first learned of the sacred practice in 1990. I was a taking a Mastery course in Hypnosis and Neuro-Linguistic Programming (NLP) on the Big Island of Hawaii led by Tad James PhD. We were introduced to Hawaiian Huna and the forgiveness process. Immediately, the chanting and internal cleaning resonated with me, and I began to feel lighter as a result. We were also visited by teachers from the Foundation of I, developed by Morrnah, who introduced the modern Ho'oponopono process to our world. What a treasure and an honor to receive this collection of self-healing wisdom before Morrnah's passing in 1992.

In her version, she made it possible for us to do the cleansing ourselves with our own Higher Self instead of having to do it as a family unit. Said Morrnah, "Clean, erase, erase and find your own Shangri-La. Where? Within yourself. The main purpose of this process is to discover the Divinity within ourselves. The Ho'oponopono is a profound gift that allows one to develop a working relationship with the Divinity within and learn to ask that in each moment, our errors in thought, word, deed or action be cleansed. The process is essentially about freedom, complete freedom from the past." (Source: Wikipedia entry for Morrnah Simeona)

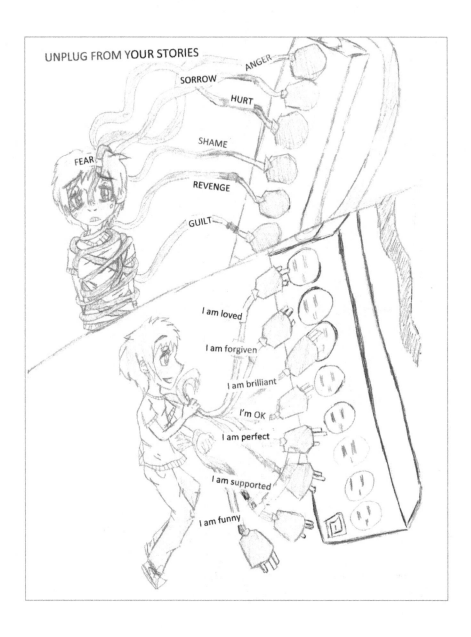

Chapter 14 – Ho'oponopono – To Make Right Again

This chapter outlines the step-by-step process when practicing Ho'oponopono.

Remember that whatever we attach to emotionally forms a cord or what has been called an "AKA connection" or an AKA cord. Emanating from your navel or belly area, the cords of discord may be invisible to the physical world, yet they are all too real in our mind, where we create so much of our reality. The Egyptians described such cords by framing the unconscious emotional mind as a sticky grasshopper that gets caught up in sticky emotions. Sir Walter Scott penned, "Oh what a tangled web we weave, when first we practice to deceive." We all know the experience of feeling tied to another person or the feeling of someone "yanking on our chain" when they trigger our emotions. When we detach or "cut the cord" or "pull the plug" we are literally dissolving our attachment to the person, experience or thing.

Unplugging from attachments or cord cutting always releases the old energy so a new higher energy can open the door to a much better event to take place ... like receiving an unexpected gift.

It should be noted that some people are invested in keeping attached to their emotional stories. They don't want to pull the plugs because these stories define who they think they are. You might hear some say, "It's my pain" or "Life did this to me and now I'm stuck with it" or "It's because of my family that I'm this way." These stuck individuals do not know how to live their lives without the limiting beliefs. They are wholly invested in the beliefs because they cannot see what would replace them.

If you are willing to let your stories end, and allow for a new world of magic to begin, then please follow these easy steps to your freedom:

1. Begin by accumulating "mana" or Life Force through a practice of deep breathing. Take a deep breath through the nose, all the way to the top of the head (where your Higher Self resides) and hold it for the count of four. Slowly let the exhale travel out through the mouth making the sound of haaaaaa as it moves down your body. You will feel your heart vibrating with the "HA breath." Do this breath in sets of four with a rest inbetween for about 10 minutes. (Or 10 sets of 4 "HA" breaths). It is ideal to build up the Life Force in your body before you cut your cords. This also prepares your unconscious mind (labeled "George" or "Unihipili") to open up the "storage house" of unresolved emotions and events that have been kept concealed within. Safe now to release the past, you are giving permission for the unconscious to finally let these past experiences and energies leave the body so the unconscious mind can give and receive more love without obstruction. Remember too, your unconscious self loves you unconditionally and will only bring up what you can handle in the moment. After all, this aspect of self continues to run your body without your conscious awareness. This breathing aspect of the process – done on its own if you are short on time – can be done repeatedly during the day to maintain a clean and clear disposition.

2. Close your eyes. Visualize, feel or mentally sense a theater stage below you. See yourself on a platform diagonally looking down upon the stage. You might choose to be outside on a platform, in a tree, or on a hillside looking down below you. Take some time to picture or sense this. You could also choose to be in a projection booth of a theatre

looking down upon a stage. The setting does not matter. It is only important that you feel comfortable creating or feeling this sense of separation between you and the stage.

3. Invite onto the stage the people with whom you wish to make amends, starting with your mother and father. Make these people quite small in stature. Even if they have passed over, you can still invite them to be present on the stage. You are mainly carrying within your mind "a concept" about these people, and these concepts have formed the "AKA cords" we wish to cut. These people are actually an extension of you.

4. Ask them this question: "Do you support me today in my connection with Higher Self?" If you feel totally supported – with no doubting dialogue or attitude – then they may leave the stage. If there is any doubt or discord within you, keep them on the stage. You may notice cords or long strings that have formed from your umbilicus to the people on the stage. These cords represent our negative perceptions and illusions about these people in our lives. Formed in the past, the illusions sustained because we did not have the tools, resources, or wisdom that we have today.

5. Next, ask your "ancestors" to come onto the stage. You may not even know these people, but you are still carrying their DNA from all the negative experiences and emotions that preceded you. Your decision to stop these energetic patterns can be enough so that it does not continue into future generations. Again, ask the question of those on stage: "Do you support me today in my connection with my Higher Self?" If you get a "yes" answer, then you may let them go. If they hesitate or give a "no" response, you can keep them on the stage.

6. To this group you will add your grandparents, brothers and sisters, aunts, uncles, cousins, nephews, nieces, stepparents, stepbrothers and sisters, step-children, as well as your

own children, grandchildren (over the age of 10 yrs. old), and anyone who served as "family." Again, ask them the question: "Do you support me today in my connection with my Higher Self?" Those with a favorable answer can go. The others remain on the stage.

7. The next group invited onto the stage includes your "exes" – ex-husband, ex-wife, ex-boyfriend, ex-girlfriend, and ex-in-laws. Follow through with the same question, perhaps adding one thought: "From the beginnings of time until now, do you support me in my connection with my Higher Self?" Often we are not aware of what the unconscious mind has been storing. So this question gives permission for all the exes to appear on the stage. Just as with the others, make the image of these people very tiny on the stage.

8. The next invitation goes to those you consider authority figures. These are people who have been teachers and mentors. Perhaps someone here took your power away from you in an inappropriate way. To whom do you give your power? You can place tangible and intangible objects down on the stage, such as: money, IRS, police, lawyers, doctors, hospitals, your job, your house, politicians, governments … whatever you give your power to that keeps depleting your energy. Follow through with the same questioning, and see what leaves the stage and what remains.

9. The next group consists of your friends (old and new ones), your present relationship (husband or wife, partner or lover), clients from your workplace with whom you feel some disharmony, anyone who has "passed over" with whom you wish to make amends, or anyone else your unconscious mind reveals to you. Ask them all the vital question: "Do you support me today in my connection with my Higher Self?"

10. The final group invited onto the stage includes the pets, plant kingdom, or unborn spirits. If you have any guilt

about an abortion or miscarriage, that guilt keeps this spirit-being locked here on the Earth plane. Place these "beings" down on the stage as well.

11. And finally put your own *self-image* down upon the stage. This is the person you perceive yourself to be, with all your judgments, obsessions and misconceptions about yourself. Anything you have said to hurt yourself has created an invisible cord that is wrapped around yourself, almost like the inside of a golf ball. This is the person you've invested your electromagnetic energy into – the one your ego has been feeding with false information and ideas. You might see yourself down on the stage with cords that represent such concepts:

- "I'm unlovable."
- "I'm too fat. I'm too skinny."
- "I'm not good enough."
- "Nobody loves me."
- "I'm worthless."

If this has been an inner dialogue, you can thank your ego, which is trying to kill the body in its own way. When picturing yourself on stage, you might look like a mummy all wrapped up in cords. Ask yourself if the investment in any negative perceptions of yourself has paid you back valuable dividends. If your answer is NO, then it is time to stop the nonsense, kick your true self into gear, and call your spirit back!

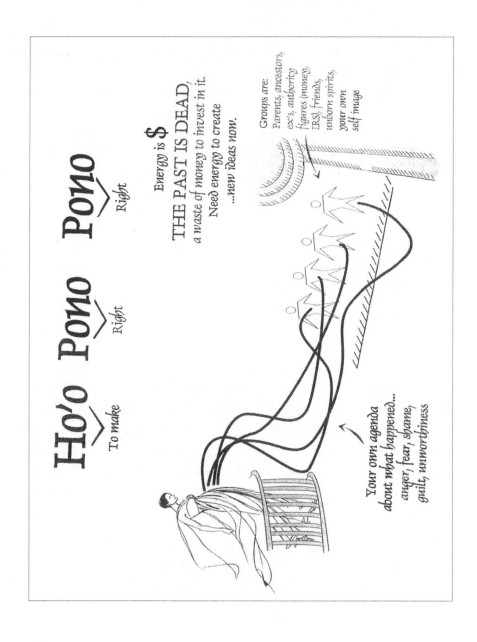

12. Using your inner vision look deep inside your unconscious mind and "spiritual body" to see if there are any dark or gray areas that have accumulated around you. This would represent dense energy that has superimposed itself over your unconscious mind when you were in a weaker state or in conflict. If you have ever used drugs, alcohol, or nicotine **excessively** in the past, or if you have not resolved a traumatic emotional experience (rape, incest, etc.), then the body weakens, and this allows "lower level" energies to be attracted into the body's force field. Envision these "dark forms" on the stage as well. It is inappropriate and unnecessary for these energies to stay with you any longer. They have misunderstood their purpose for being here. When given the chance, parts of the self, desire to evolve to a higher level. They are only stuck here until a guide arrives to take them to the Light. By using the CD *Chant and Forgiveness*, listeners are guided with the chants to send these dense energies to the Light where they will evolve to a higher form. To allow the denser energies to remain with you only delays your own evolution, as well as their ascendance to a higher level of being. If you do not have access to the CD, you can ask these energies to leave the space, in the name of the Light. Ask them to leave because it is their time. You can say, "Thy will be done for the greatest good of all, thank you God." Ask them to leave on behalf of your Higher Self. It's been said that faith the size of a mustard seed can move mountains. Know that your strong intention to send them to the Light is the prayer that will light their way. Your Higher Self will do it for you.

13. Take a deep breath and imagine an infinite source of Light, Love, and Healing originating from the top of your head, flowing down through your mind and heart and sending it to all the people on the stage, even the dark forms, until they are completely surrounded with this Light. This is

the Light that comes from your Higher Self down to their Higher Selves. Remember, everyone has a Higher Self.

14. Now prepare to have an inner dialogue with these energies, people and stage dwellers. It can be as simple as saying, "I forgive you" or "I love you." Ask your Higher Self to do this for you. Ask and you shall receive. It can be done very quickly. **The person you are forgiving is yourself.** As I say these words, I do a "shimmy shake" of my body, like that of a duck flapping its wings. The shake corresponds to the dissolving of connections with those people and events down on the stage.

81

15. Once your brief dialogue is complete, take a cutting instrument of your choice: a knife, scissors, chain saw, blades from your Higher Self, and spin this cutting instrument around you so that the cords dissolve between you and those images on the stage. Next watch or feel these images float away. You can also say, again, "Thy will be done for the greatest good of all," a statement which returns them to a Higher Power. I have found that some people "cut cords" out of anger, but this only forms new cords because it is not done with the Higher Self. Make sure to cut cords out of the highest intention of freedom and harmony. Instead of using the word "cut" you can also use the word "dissolve" or "unplug" – but use whatever works best for your mind in seeing and feeling the dissolution of the cord.

16. Know that you may have leftover cords after your cutting, perhaps emanating from your belly area and dangling free. It's important to tuck the leftover cords back inside your ethereal self, for you will need all of your energy for your own wellbeing. By doing the ceremonial cutting, you are literally unplugging yourself from your mental agenda with these people. Your process will be complete for now.

Ho'o Pono Pono

To make · Right · Right · Right

Breathe down LIGHT from YOUR Higher Self to THEIR Higher Selves.

The Light from your breath (Higher Self) melts the dark cords into Light before you cut the cords. Then use a cutting instrument (knife, scissors, blades from your Higher Self) to cut the cords counterclockwise. Tuck leftover cords back inside yourself.

Watch or sense the people float away. They will reconnect to you at a higher level. You can never cut the Divine Cord of Love. You are only cutting your own agenda with them

Person you are forgiving is YOURSELF

As you do your process, you will come to realize that it has been your agenda and mental concepts around these people that has been the true conflict, not the actual people. Your mental constructs have been your perceptions and stories. This is what has been bothering and hindering you this entire time. It is time to let them go. It has been in your power the entire time. Like Dorothy, in *The Wizard of Oz*, who wanted to get back to Kansas, you have always had the power to return to grace and innocence. You will be able to retain the love for the people in your life. Everything else – a mere perception or an illusion of separation – is what will be released. The mystery will be solved and the magic will return. The mystery underneath it all is that the person you are actually forgiving is yourself. How's that for an eye opener?

Know that if a person remains on the stage or still holds a negative charge, there is something within yourself that is not ready to let go. You may not be ready to forgive yourself about the perception you hold about this person or event. If you want to raise your frequency and move forward, then again see them down on the stage. Take a deep breath to the top of your head and ask the Higher Self to send down the Infinite Source of Light and Healing to this person or "extension of self." Spin the cutting instrument around you and let them go. You can shake your body and turn your right arm upward signifying their departure. When you meet with this person or any of the others, you will be able to deal with whatever issues you have between you from a higher perspective. By dissolving your cords, the problem usually resolves itself and the problem disappears. I have had it happen on more than one occasion where the person who held discord with me calls to apologize in the following days after I do the practice.

And when can you do this process? It is recommended that you cleanse yourself daily, using the Ho'oponopono, to call your spirit back and return to present time. Just like a regular ritual, I dissolve my cords every night when I take a bath. All my negative thoughts for the day go down the drain. The ancient Hawaiians usually cut their cords at sunset, letting their thought-forms dissolve down into the water with the Sun. You can do it anytime. This is a personal choice. Sometimes it's necessary to do it in the middle of the day when you might get upset over something. Instead of letting it fester inside of you, forgive yourself and let it go.

Remember – You are a Being of Light and you DO deserve forgiveness. Call your Spirit back. As a Being of Light you are a channel for that Light. Clearing yourself from your past allows you to feel lighter and more in touch with that luminosity. You have a mission in this lifetime to return to the heartfelt love inside of you – you deserve to receive Divine Love. Raise your vibrations and welcome home the Mother/Father/Spirit love into your heart to comfort you. The shift now taking place on this planet in the 21st Century requires us more than ever to open our hearts to its natural state. Do not hold back. Do not hide away. Do not be a sissy. It is time, for you, for us, for all on our planet. We are all counting on you.

CHAPTER 15 – RECONNECTIVE HEALING

After my son died and my income money was lost, my ability to help others heal was put on hold. I couldn't heal my way out of a paper bag. For one thing, I needed all my energy to sell my furniture, jewelry and anything else to make a rent payment and adapt to a different lifestyle. I moved in with my daughter Jessica and son-in-law and took over the childcare of my grandson Eddie who was three years old. Taking care of Eddie fed my soul. I would look forward to the patter of his little feet coming to play with me in the morning. During this period I was so grateful to have a roof over my head and to feel needed by another. My low self-esteem and unbearable grief needed a boost. I continued to do the Ho'oponopono process, forgiving myself for the way I had interpreted what had happened to my son and to my income. As I kept unplugging from the way I was looking at my situation, it started to change. So each time I cut my cords, I felt better, lighter and one step further into my healing.

After a few months of living with my daughter, I was invited by my good friends, Simant and Patty, to see a special presentation of the film *The Living Matrix*, a film on the New Science of Healing. I was not very anxious to see another "blah blah presentation," but I went to it anyway since I wanted to be with my friends. As the movie opened with Dr. Eric Pearl, I was riveted to see him working on a young Greek child who was confined to a wheelchair from cerebral palsy. The mother had heard about Eric's work with "Reconnective Healing" and what they call "The Reconnection." After the first session with Eric, the child jumped off the couch. After several more sessions, he was able to play on the playground with other children.

With every cell of my body, I knew I wanted to learn what Eric was doing to help this child heal. It was the same "ah-ha" moment I had when I first learned about Huna almost 20 years before. It was like finding the missing piece to a puzzle that you've been working on forever. I came home that night and Googled "The Reconnection." I found out when and where I could learn this method. Eric was teaching in Chicago in two weeks, and I immediately registered for the course.

I found a practitioner in Santa Cruz to give me a session so I could experience the healing for myself. After my first session, which took about 40 minutes, I definitely felt lighter. In fact, I remember feeling downright joyful. Now there's a feeling I had not experienced since my son's passing. It was like this huge anchor had been lifted from my chest. To me it was a miracle that I could not explain. Even with my regular cord cutting, there was still unconscious grief I was carrying. Amazingly, one Reconnective Healing session took all my grief away. This is not to say that I still don't get sad considering my son's passing, but the heaviness I was experiencing was definitely lifted. I was ecstatic beyond belief.

Before leaving for my training, I had the unfortunate experience of falling off my bike and breaking my left wrist. Of course, it felt like the worst timing ever. But how do we know the "accidents" in our lives are not simply blessings in disguise? At the time, I didn't see it because I felt so incredibly inconvenienced. I did not see a doctor because I had no medical insurance. Using all my healing tools, I went to work on healing the wrist by talking to it directly and reminding it, "you remember how to heal and be strong again." I also said, "I'm sorry, I love you" over and over again. In addition, I went back for two more Reconnective Healing sessions to speed up the recovery. And it helped so very much.

A Reconnective Healing session will give the person exactly what they need to balance themselves emotionally, physically, mentally, and spiritually. You need not "target" something specific to heal. The frequencies know exactly what you need at the time. For the case of my wrist, it improved but was still far from being fully functional. I decided to have the same practitioner do the 2-day Reconnection on me before I traveled to Chicago for my training. By the time I got to Chicago, my wrist was fine.

Another example of healing using the Reconnective Healing process came about because of a thyroid issue. It took two years for a thyroid problem to manifest because the feelings that created the issue ran so deep. During a routine checkup, my acupuncturist was feeling my throat and came across "a suspicious lump" on my neck. Naturally, that is not the news one expects to hear. It seemed to be underneath a muscle because it was not visible to the naked eye. I also had some suspicious hoarseness. A biopsy revealed that it was a 4-inch long tumor on my thyroid. It was benign, thank goodness. I looked up the mental cause for the physical illness of my thyroid in Louise Hay's book, *Heal Your Body*. It had been growing for the past two years, ever since I experienced the devastating loss of my income investment. Hmmmm.

Even though I was making the best of a bad situation, living with my daughter and playing with my grandson, I must have deeply felt humiliated at losing the money, and it is this emotional energy that created the tumor on my thyroid. Losing a lot of money is not something one is particularly proud of. So deep down that humiliation was felt by my unconscious mind, and this had a direct effect on my physical body. My unconscious mind followed the direction of my emotion that manifested the tumor.

Once I knew what I had created, I went to my Internet and Googled "thyroid" to see what it looked like. I was happy to find out that it resembled the shape of a butterfly – one of my favorite symbols. I quickly found a blue butterfly – blue being the color of the throat chakra - and placed it on the wall in front of me so I could constantly breathe in the shape and energy of a healthy thyroid again. Because the unconscious is like a 2-year-old child, it needs symbols to comprehend.

I touched my neck lovingly with my hand and thanked the tumor for being there. Like a 2-year-old child, it must first feel accepted before it can change. A year later I returned to the specialist for a follow up. The tumor had flattened and shrunk an inch. It was even difficult to find. The doctor looked at me and said, "These tumors don't go away." Of course, I obviously said that this would be an exception. As I left the office the doctor said that I was "medically boring," which I took as a compliment. I was also doing the Ho'oponopono and forgiving myself for feeling the humiliation around my losses. By taking responsibility for creating the symptoms in my body and doing these procedures, my body is returning back to healthy wholeness.

This Reconnective Healing process is truly a gift to our world, and for anyone who comes to learn it and facilitate it. And who is it that is trained in Reconnective Healing? At my training, I met housewives, health practitioners, acupuncturists, dental hygienists, lawyers, accountants, osteopaths, ER doctors, and many more in all walks of life. One woman wanted to learn how to heal her husband from a terminal illness. Another person was there with her daughter in a wheelchair hoping to pass on the healing directly to her daughter. We heard over and over that "this is not a technique nor is it energy." Energy dissipates when you walk away. Yet these frequencies of Light grow stronger the further away you are from them.

Scientists have measured these frequencies. I personally did a 20-minute session for a gentleman who was hooked up to an Aura Imaging Machine. His aura color had always photographed in the red colors, which meant that he was functioning at the 3rd dimension or primitive basic survival level. As I started finding the frequencies around him and stretching them out, the red color shifted to yellows and greens. By the time we ended at 20 minutes, his aura took on blues and lavender and purple. He was stunned by the shift in his body. It also validated to me the power of this "HANDS OFF healing" work.

So how can we explain this healing work? We must go back in time, back to when we all became disconnected from the Source. As humans we've been flagellating ourselves here on Earth allowing ourselves to feel separate and unworthy. The Reconnection accelerates us on our life path and true purpose in life by aligning us with the true purpose of our Higher Self.

The client lies on the massage table and receives the Light and Information coming in. The facilitator simply feels, finds, and stretches the frequencies around the body. The practitioner serves as a 3rd-party filter to the client and their Higher Self. It is such an honor to be a part of this Trinity.

I am convinced I would not be writing this book now if I had not had my Reconnection done. During the training in Chicago, my wrist felt 100 percent better. There were 150 people all using the Reconnective Healing in one room. Without special attention, my wrist felt like it was being electrically charged by healing Light. Thank goodness it healed because I needed my wrist in order to practice the Reconnective Healing on other participants. After my training in Chicago completing Levels 1, 2, and 3, I returned to Santa Cruz recharged and ready to share these healing frequencies with others. I was so motivated and inspired by the results.

I've now done hundreds of Reconnective Healing sessions in Santa Cruz, Carmel, Monterey, Los Angeles and Hawaii. The common thread running through many sessions is hearing the client say they felt like electricity is running through them, especially in the areas that are problematic. Many clients see colors and even feel that someone is touching them. As the practitioner, I do not target any area or ask about any history. In fact, the less I know about the client the better. Without an agenda, the frequencies are able to give the client more than what they even think they need. If they get an unexpected healing ... then all the better. One client told me, a month after her session, that she no longer "crashes" after working a full day. She has much more energy and lightness, which opens the door to having more fun in her life. This was huge for her because she would have to sleep for hours to recover from normal activities. Another client was able to "swim freely" again using both arms, which was impressive because one of her arms had been uncomfortably frozen for about a year.

Another interesting story with a Reconnective Healing happened with a client who admitted to me that she "was too mental" and wished she could "feel more." She was always in her head. Right after the sessions, she called me with real fear because she was able to finally feel her fears and the issues going on in her family. These real feelings were so foreign to her she didn't know how to respond to them. She and I did some Ho'oponopono over the phone to let go of the way she was looking at herself, and she felt better. Then at work, she found herself being more honest with her boss regarding company policy. Her first thought was he would fire her for her outspokenness. On the contrary, he promoted her and gave her a leadership position and a raise! Heavens to Betsy, she was elated, surprised and empowered. It was amazing to see her transformation after her Reconnective Healing session and The Reconnection. For another amazing transformation, read the testimonial below by a client I worked on, Ty Fiske.

MY MIRACLE (A Testimonial by Ty Fiske, Chandler, AZ.)

On Saturday, October 9, 2010 something miraculous and life changing happened to me. I was at the Hilton Hotel in downtown Los Angeles, California attending the 8th Annual U.S. Mastery Conference presented by "The Reconnection" when I was asked by the lady sitting next to me if I would like to receive a healing. The lady's name is Belinda Farrell and she is a Reconnective Healing practitioner. I was in a lot of pain at the time so I gratefully accepted Belinda's offer. The healing I received was faster and more powerful than I had ever imagined it would be. At the end of my 30-minute healing session I immediately felt some relief from the pain I was experiencing in my back, shoulders and neck. During the remainder of the conference my pain continued to diminish. Over a period of days and weeks the pain progressively subsided to the point that now in January of 2011 my back, shoulder and neck pain is completely gone.

MY CONDITION

I had been visiting a chiropractor twice a week during most of 2010 for problems I was having with my back, shoulders, neck and one foot. I have always had a very bad posture so I walked somewhat slumped over. I injured my back a number of times snow skiing, jet skiing and quading on large sand dunes. To compound my problems I injured my back twice at work. The result was lots of pain in my back and shoulders. I was diagnosed with dual curvatures of the spine. I had continual pain in my neck and it was very painful to turn my head to the left. When I drove my car, I had to turn my entire body to look left before changing lanes because of the pain and loss of movement in my neck. I was diagnosed with arthritis in my neck and was told that it was permanent. I was born with very flat feet and I have been wearing custom orthotics for many years. In 2010 the big toe of my left foot started feeling like it was broken when I walked. The diagnosis was the ligaments going across the arch from the toe to the heel were stretched causing a bone behind the big toe to protrude up. The result was pain in my big toe every time I took a step.

MY HEALING

Belinda told me to lie down with my head at the foot of the bed, arms at my side with my eyes closed. She told me to relax and just observe any sensations I may experience during the healing. The Reconnective Healing she facilitated was hands off, so she never touched me during the 30 minutes it took. I started to feel the first sensation soon after she began. I felt pain starting to build in my spine from my shoulders down my back for about 2 and half feet. The pain grew more and more intense during an approximately 30 second period and then quickly subsided. A few seconds later I began to feel the second sensation. I felt pain developing in a 6-inch line from the inside of my left wrist and up my arm. It grew more intense for about 20 seconds and then quickly subsided. A number of minutes went by before the third sensation began.

The best way I can describe the sensation is "all of a sudden my sinuses popped open". Before this happened my sinuses were already completely open and I was breathing normally, yet I had that sensation of the massive opening of my sinuses to the point that I thought the capillaries in my nose were going to burst, and I was going to have a nose bleed. Thankfully that did not happen, but I had never before felt my sinuses open to that degree. The fourth sensation began immediately. I started to feel pain in the center of my forehead just above my eyes. The pain slowly increased over a 30-second period and got very intense. While I was experiencing this pain, it started to migrate to the right, across my forehead to the side of my head. At this point the pain quickly went away and Belinda immediately tapped me on the shoulder and told me we were finished. The pain I felt during my healing was not uncomfortable. In fact it actually felt good, maybe because I knew I was being healed. Belinda offered her description of my sensations as not pain but intense pressure.

MY INTERPRETATION

The pain I was experiencing in my spine during the healing was the start of my back, shoulders and neck injuries being healed, and my life-long dual curvatures of the spine being corrected. At that moment the ongoing healing of these conditions was set into motion. The 6-inch line of pain in my arm during the healing was in perfect line with my index finger. In 2006 I accidentally severed the end of that finger and it was reattached. I have not yet felt any changes in that finger. The pain I experienced in my forehead was the opening of my third eye and a massive amount of light and information being downloaded in an extremely short period of time.

MY FOOT

I received the miraculous healing during the seminar lunch break. That evening after returning to my hotel room, I had taken a shower and was standing barefoot on the carpet when I felt a very strange sensation. It felt like something was under my skin chewing on the inside arch of my left foot. The first thought that popped into my mind was that a big bug, like a large cockroach or something even worse, was chewing on my bare foot. I immediately grabbed my foot and rubbed it.

I was relieved that there was nothing there. The sensation quickly went away so I put my foot down. About 5 seconds later I felt the same sensation return. I grabbed my foot again because it felt so real. I rubbed it again and the sensation quickly went away. This happened 2 or 3 more times until it finally stopped. Since that time, the pain in my big toe has progressively been subsiding and is now almost completely gone. I thought to myself "what is a miracle?" so I Googled it.

A miracle is: "An extraordinary event manifesting a supernatural work of God."

CHAPTER 16 – CLEARING ENTITIES AND DE-POSSESSION

There is a lot of misconception about "entities" thanks to Hollywood's portrayal of them in movies such as "The Exorcist." In all the years I've been helping my clients to "de-possess of entities," I never saw a head spin around or green spit-up on my watch, although I did witness some pretty big bugs crawl out of one client's ear.

The premise behind "entities" in the Hawaiian tradition is that they are "thought forms" pure and simple. If you invest in the same belief over and over again, your energy will create that thought into form. If you were of the belief that spirits could inhabit your body, then they will. It would be as though you invited them inside. Once attached to the living, these spirits could create physical or mental illness. According to Max Freedom Long's book *The Secret Science at Work,* these spirits draw Life Force (mana) from the living and are called "eating companions." To remove them, the kahuna would accumulate a lot of mana through breathing and chanting to reach the Higher Self of the patient, and then give a hypnotic suggestion that would dislodge the unwanted spirit, sending it into the Light.

According to Huna beliefs, there is no reference to an ill person as being "bad" or "filled with the devil." What you would find in the teachings is a person who possessed a large amount of darkness as opposed to Light. Breaking down the darkness allows it to dissipate into Light. After all, everything is energy in one form or another. Light is considered to be Supreme Intelligence and Good. Darkness is lack of intelligence, stupidity, and all that would oppose Light.

When I first started to learn about de-possession in Hawaii back in the 1990's, I was told not to do the de-possessions along with Ho'oponopono until I was initiated into the "protection symbols." That would mean that I had to wait for several months. Patience was not my strong trait at that time. Also, I was extremely motivated to help people recover from their illnesses. So I went ahead and accepted a client that had severe Parkinson's disease. In order to sit him still in my healing chair, I had to physically hold his arm down myself. After that session I ended up being in bed myself for three days with a fever of 104 degrees. Some energy definitely had transferred from my client and was draining me. I was certainly a believer in "protection" after that. Never did that happen to me again.

Another de-possession story involved a gentleman (Jeff from page 31) who called me and wanted me to make a "house call" to rid him of an entity that had been with him since childhood. While he was driving one day, he said he taunted "the entity" and this resulted in a collision with a trailer truck, leaving him a quadriplegic. I did not usually make house calls, but there was no other way we could get together. Jeff wanted me to come in person. I arrived at his building and proceeded to "clean" his place energetically by chanting the ancient Hawaiian chants. Once I felt comfortable, we got started. It was apparent that this "entity" had been taunting Jeff ever since childhood. Who knows why these things attach to some people. But it usually happens when the person is in a weakened state. When he was in the car, Jeff challenged the spirit to come for him. Jeff got his wish in the form of a tragic crash, which left him a quadriplegic.

Before we started the session, Jeff wanted to make sure I understood that he did not want to be healed with the gift of walking again. He liked his life the way it was. He only requested that the entity be removed. I started to talk to the entity in Hawaiian using an authoritative voice. Nothing happened. Then I spoke softer and started to chant. This "rattles the cage" of whatever is inside that is not of the Light. The particular chant I used asks for the darkness to leave and be replaced with Light. Protection is provided to the entity as it moves towards the Light. I chanted over and over again, using a softer voice, directing my focus on Jeff's body. Believe it or not, within the hour, we both saw the entity lifting up and out away from Jeff. The entity was dressed in a tap dancer's black coat and tails, wearing a black top hat, carrying a cane and tap dancing. I know this must sound unbelievable, but Jeff and I both saw him and looked at one another in utter amazement. After this, Jeff's body completely relaxed. He was so grateful that he could finally say goodbye to this childhood trauma. He was finally at peace, and that's all that matters.

Kathy and Paul, a married couple, were scheduled to come together for a de-possession session. Kathy wanted her husband to go first so I complied. Paul admitted that he could not sleep at night and was bothered by recurring nightmares. When we started the session, he was very agitated and scared. Usually chanting comforts the client, but Paul was beyond comforting. I sensed an enormous amount of guilt at the root level. By the time we started the forgiveness process of unplugging from his negative attachments, Paul started hyperventilating and he was convinced that "the army was coming to get me for all my wrongdoings." "What did you do wrong?" I asked. "I killed children, I'm so evil" he blurted out crying. I kept chanting because by that time, I was getting more than concerned. His face became bright red and began to take on the characteristics of Adolph Hitler. His moustache was identical to that worn by the dictator. I told him that he had to face the army and tell them "I am sorry, please forgive me." He wanted to look away and run. But I convinced him to face the army, which actually caused the army to stop in their tracks and finally melt away. Remember fear as "False Evidence Appearing Real." It was definitely real to Paul and his sleep was interrupted because of it. After some time, Paul finally relaxed and stopped shaking. I do believe he created this army out of guilt from his past. When I checked back with Paul, he was grateful that his sleeping had improved.

CHAPTER 17 – MANTRAS, CHANTING AND FREEDOM

Since the conscious mind communicates with the unconscious mind constantly, we must consider the tremendous influence we hold in guiding our thoughts. We do have the power to give input to our unconscious mind, which in turn runs much of our day-to-day manifestations. Monks and followers of spiritual teachings know this truth and routinely recite prayers or "mantras" all through the day to focus their thoughts. Even saying the words, "I love you, I forgive you, thank you" – noted in the Ho'oponopono forgiveness process – provides a constant flow of loving frequencies between the conscious and unconscious mind.

Words are so powerful. Ever since my spine healed from complete degeneration so beautifully 15 years ago, I've been thanking my back for supporting me and for remembering how to regenerate. Of course, I've had challenges since then. I recently woke up with lower back pain and didn't know where it came from. But I remembered I had not been stretching lately or been disciplined with exercises. I started to apologize to my back, touching it gently, and speaking to it like you would a wounded child. After a few days, my back felt completely relieved. Even my daughter has gotten into that habit. Now that she's become a marathon runner, she admitted to me that she's been "talking to her ankles and knees" lately while running. To her amazement, she's feeling a powerful connection and relief.

The power of words is even more charged with the use of "mantras," or sacred chants we repeat in order to gain connection with a higher mind in meditation. I was given my first special mantra almost 20 years ago from the sacred Indian Mother, Ammachi. She was visiting San Ramon, California on her compassionate hugging tour. My son and I stayed with her for three days receiving hugs, volunteering at the ashram, and learning the importance of mantras. She gave me a mantra that I recite daily, hold dear to my heart and say with great reverence. It helps me focus my mind, calm my spirit and connect me with what is truly important in life. I suggest you find a way to manifest in your life your own mantra for the power it can bring to you.

In my dear Hawaii, the ancient wisdom knew of the power found in language. The Hawaiian language is very simple because it has only seven consonants as compared to English with 21. So there are many ways to say the same thing allowing for different interpretations. If you look at a Hawaiian dictionary there can be 12 or more meanings for the same word. If you are serious about learning the chants found in Hawaiian culture, here is the simple vowel pronunciation:

- A is pronounced ah, ' ala
- U is pronounced as in you, ooo, 'ulu
- E is pronounced eh ' ele
- W is pronounced like a "va" sound
- I is pronounced 'eee, 'ili
- Au is pronounced ow, as in " ouch"
- O is pronounced oh, 'olo
- Ai is pronounced as in "eye"

The ancient Hawaiian chants evoke powerful sounds that awaken the DNA of our sleeping cells. English is too young a language to evoke the same feeling. Listening to the chants, one could say that the person listening feels awakened at a deeper level. As a chanter, I feel the chants originate in my heart chakra, transforming me and those who listen in. I am also told that it is not simply me alone doing the chanting, but also the lineage of the hundreds of chanters who chanted that particular chant before me. This is why the vibrations of the chants resonate deeper, almost from another time and place. Many times when I have been on an airplane during a storm or bumpy weather, I begin to chant the "Ho'opuka" chant. Almost immediately, I feel calmness within myself. Each time the weather has cleared and the ride has become smooth again. On one such turbulent ride, my daughter was sitting next to me looking out the window. She was the first to see the Sun bursting through the clouds. She whispered to me, "I have to learn that chant, Mom."

They say one such amazing Hawaiian chant has the power to evoke a total sense of peacefulness to the chanter and to the ones listening to the chant. One of the most amazing chants of all: "NOHO ANA KE AKUA PULE O KANE."

Ai Noho Ana Keakua I ka na helehele

I alai ia e ke ki ohu ohu e ka ua koko

E na kino malu I ka lani

Malu e hoe

E ho 'o ulu mai ana o Kane I Kona Kahu

Owau 'owau noa ua I kea.

Arouse us, like the rising of the sea, your Life Force like rain falling comes to us and we are free. The peacefulness, like spiritual food, continues to flow over us with the breath. Oh, Infinite Protector, come towards us and satisfy us until we are fulfilled. We become as you are as the darkness is lifted. We are freed from fears and restrictions bathing only in the infinite rain of your Light.

This chant – featured on CD's *Chant and Forgiveness; A Huna Odyssey*, and *EnCHANTment* – asks the Higher Self, also known as "Kane," to come quickly from above the top of our heads, and move inside us to comfort and sooth us. I've been asked to recite it during an opening ceremony at conventions, on the radio, and as a protection in the face of imminent danger. One such example of the protection factor was clearly experienced in Hawaii with my Huna group. We were about to enter the ocean one morning to swim with the dolphins when a threatening gentleman, whom we called "the dolphin police," approached my group warning us in an angry tone not to swim with the dolphins. He towered over me in height. I immediately started chanting up to him. He was speechless and seemed paralyzed when he heard the sound of the chant.

Then he turned and walked away never bothering us again. My group was stunned and became believers in the power of these frequencies to change the heart and mind.

Frequently, I will play my CD *EnCHANTment* in the car when my 6 year old grandson is riding with me. Nothing like getting them started early to listen to these sounds. Eddie gets very quiet when the Ai Noho Ana Chant comes on. On one occasion, he said "That singing makes me feel like **nothing**—I like it."

That particular chant also works magic with animals. In 2000 I traveled to Peru and Machu Picchu as a guest speaker with Power Places Tours. I started chanting to some wild llamas when one walked over to me and planted a kiss on my mouth. Someone captured that Kodak moment which is my most cherished picture. Another incident happened the next year in Bali. We were at a public zoo featuring a Komodo dragon. For some reason the dragon had been hiding in his bushes for several days. I started to do this chant and out came the dragon right up to our fenced-in enclosure. He looked up at me with his gigantic tongue waving back and forth in his mouth. What a thrill that was for all of us there. Again, the picture speaks for itself. The animals are enchanted with the frequency of the chant.

Fortunately, you do not have to learn complicated chants to enjoy the benefit of chanting. For example, laughter is the chant of the heart. Hahahahahahahahahahahaha. That's right, the simple HA sound can fill the air with laughter and the HA breath. Listen to children laughing and observe the joy they feel. You don't even need to have something to laugh about. It's just a muscle. You can force the HA sound from your chest in the beginning. And after a bit, I'll bet you'll keep on laughing and inspire those around you to laugh as well. I remember a YouTube video of a man getting onto a train, which held some pretty depressed looking passengers. The man started smiling and then laughing for no reason. Soon the laughter was contagious and spread throughout the train. When the man got off the passengers were still laughing. What a gift he gave to them. As they say, laughter is definitely good medicine. In fact, a good way to call the wild dolphins in the water is to begin laughing. Out of nowhere, the dolphins appear summoned by the joy frequency that laughter carries. Just recently, I was swimming with two friends, Cecily and Celeste, in Hawaii. It was Cecily's birthday, and we began to sing to her in the water. As we finished, we looked up and saw a nursery pod of dolphins coming towards us. A dolphin had just been born, so we sang "happy birthday" to the new baby. What a gift this was for Cecily and all of us on this special day!

Chapter 18 – The Higher Self / The God Self

Consciously connecting to my Higher Self for the first time happened during a breathing exercise in Hawaii in the early 90's. Lying on the floor with other participants, I was breathing deeply in sets of 4 for 10 minutes or longer. Suddenly, I felt a rush of warm energy at the top of my head. I saw oceans parting and pods of dolphins and whales filling in all the watery spaces.

This experience was so foreign to me because dolphins and whales had never been on my radar because of my lifelong fear of water. Curious at this unusual spectacle, I welcomed in these beings like a long-awaited floodgate had opened.

That night my dreams were filled with dolphins teaching me how to swim. It was effortless, like I was one of them playing, swirling, jumping, chirping, making love, blowing bubbles and feeling free. The dreams continued until I finally got the message that they were calling me to come out to the ocean and meet them. They opened the door. It was up to me to walk through.

Swimming with them for the past 20 years is like being in the presence of higher frequencies. We have traveled through portals and other dimensions together. They have allowed me to feel deeply and experience clarity of thought. They have been and continue to be a connection to my Higher Self.

This past trip in 2012, I was swimming out by myself early in the morning in one of the sacred Bays in Hawaii when I heard the sonar loud and clear. Suddenly, I was surrounded by 50 to 60 dolphins, ranging from newborn to adult, caught up in a frenzy of jubilation.

But unlike the dreams of my past, this experience was real. No longer scared of the water and my emotions, I dove deeper into the clear blue aqua waters with these Divine Beings joining in their celebration. At the end of this joyous celebration, I was gifted by one dolphin sending me two enormous bubbles (said to be filled with Light and Information). I thanked them and swam back to shore barely able to process what just happened. I remember saying to myself, "I am baked." I can only describe this as a feeling of total completion and ultimate bliss. If I were taking drugs…this would be my drug of choice!

Even with such personal experiences, some may not believe in a Higher Self. After all, how can you prove it scientifically? I have several scientifically oriented friends who only trust modern medicine to heal them and would not think they could heal themselves. There is nothing wrong with this belief. Whatever you believe in with **all your heart** will work for you. But if you want to "explore" and "experiment" with the deeper meaning of the words "physician heal thyself," then belief in your own Higher Self as a divine source must be called upon. Faith and belief are the essential ingredients you must have to convince your low self or unconscious mind of your heart's desires: better health, changing a phobia, bringing in more wealth, etc. If you only say "positive mantras" without the inner belief and faith, then your unconscious does not bother to send your desires to the Higher Self for manifestation.

I am proof-positive that this works since my injured spine healed within days of practicing the "HA breathing prayer."

Delving deeper into the meaning of two very important Hawaiian words, we can see the importance of remembering the magic of the HA breath. So that we always remember the HA, it has been included in two very sacred words: "ALOHA" and "HAWAII." If we take apart the word "Aloha," "alo" means "in the presence of" and "ha" designates the "Divine Higher Self." It is like saying, "The Higher Self in me salutes the Higher Self in you," not unlike the Sanskrit word of "Namaste." Going deeper into the word "Hawaii," we see that "wai" means "water" or "Life Force," and "i" means the supreme. So taken together the term comes to mean: "The supreme Life Force that rides on the HA breath."

Here we have found another missing link revealed. AH HA! We have found the key! It's been here in the "aha" the entire time. Even our laughter – hahahahaha – carries the supreme connection to source, and it's this power we require when healing ourselves: mentally, emotionally and physically.

As I mentioned before, the pipeline to the Higher Self must also be cleansed of old memories (cords) to allow the "new desires" to flow upward to the Higher Self. As you continue breathing the Ha Breath in sets of 4, the unconscious will open the box of unconscious emotions to allow stuck memories to surface so that you can see them for what they truly are, learn from the experience, and release them into the ethers.

Confined to bed during the time of my paralysis, I continued to take an active role in my healing. In addition to doing concentrated breath work, I also took a homeopathic dose of snake venom, administered by a local osteopath, which helps the spine release memories.

Instantly, I could experience a baby being thrown out into the Universe like a piece of garbage. This innocent little baby, all curled up in the fetal position, was darting between asteroids and comets moving faster than the speed of Light. My heart quickened. Sweat poured down my face. I thought I was dying. Then I saw a comforting pair of hands reach down to pick up the baby and place her in the arms of a glowing figure dressed in flowing iridescent blue Lights. We were high above a precipice looking down on the mass chaos of rocks colliding into one another. The baby was safe at last. My heart was still palpitating as I tried to make sense out of that experience. I later confronted my mother to tell me the truth about my birth. She finally admitted that my father had taken her to 3 abortion clinics against her wishes. For whatever reason, thanks to Divine Intervention, attempts at aborting me failed. Yahoo!!! Yet the memory of the fetus experience was lodged within my spine and released during the breathing exercise. My unconscious had finally released the memory from "Pandora's box" because I was ready to let it go. The pathway to my Higher Self was finally cleared.

With the power of the HA breath empowering me during my time of physical challenge, I practiced over and over again seeing myself "climbing trees" with a flexible and healed spine. I accumulated the

Life Force in my unconscious mind, which sent the thought-form up to my Higher Self, which brought it down within my physical body. The unconscious is the seat of your emotions so you must "feel emotionally" the desire you want achieved – you can't just think it mentally. Empty words are not enough.

The healing secrets of the ancient Hawaiians noted the importance of the conscious mind, the unconscious mind and the Higher Self working together. All three must work together as a **team** for effectiveness. In our modern day society, people don't take the time to sit still to quiet the mind. To generate fuel for an effective prayer, your mind must be at rest so you can plant the seeds in the unconscious. If the unconscious is too active, then it will not accept the suggestion from the conscious mind. The unconscious mind is like a computer, holding the data from the conscious mind, and having the direct link to the Higher Self.

Our Higher Self can be defined as an "utterly trustworthy parental spirit" according to Hawaiian lore. We can trust our Higher Self to work with our conscious and unconscious minds to fulfill our heart's desires. The Higher Self can only work with the unconscious mind. The conscious mind has NO connection with the Higher Self. It only influences the unconscious. When there is cooperation between the conscious mind and the unconscious, then the unconscious is ready to accept the seeds of desire and send them along to the Higher Self for activation.

You may want to begin to see ways you can "lighten your load" literally. Maybe you are long overdue for a colon cleanse. Your closets haven't been sorted out in decades. Maybe your garden needs weeding. Today my sink was clogged, and I looked at that as a symbol that I needed to do some inner cleansing. Sure enough, when you unplug from your outer world, something magical happens to you on the inside.

It is best to sit and relax before starting to accumulate your extra Life Force or mana with your unconscious mind. You'll talk to it like a child. You'll tell it "Now we can begin to gather extra mana by my breathing deeply." Max Freedom Long suggests you visualize filling a jar with water or imagine a ball of light that grows bigger with each breath. You'll breathe in sets of four HA breaths. The kahunas called this the "HA Breath Rite." The sound of HA meant you were breathing strongly to reach the Higher Self. After a set of four HA breaths you will rest for the count of four so you will not pass out or become light-headed. You can breathe this way for 10-15 minutes or 10 sets of four HA breaths. You may feel more energized taking on this accumulation of mana. The beauty in this ritual is that you can do it anywhere. You can be driving your car and take in these deep breaths. Once you have this surcharge of mana, then you can send your desire up to your Higher Self.

When the ancient Hawaiians observed the missionaries recite a prayer quickly and say "amen" without sending any surcharge of mana, they would say that the prayers were not strong. They called the missionaries "Ha-ole" which means "without breath." Even today, the white people are still called breathless ones because their prayers do not have the vital force to send to the Higher Self.

Here are the steps you will use to begin your communication with the unconscious:

- DECIDE WHAT YOU REALLY WANT. (Create a blank page to write suggestions)
- RELAX YOUR UNCONSCIOUS SO IT WILL LISTEN TO YOUR DESIRES.
- DO THE HA BREATHING FOR 10-15 MINUTES or 10 sets of four HA breaths (a practice found on the CD *EnCHANTment*).
- SPEAK THE SUGGESTION TO YOUR LOW SELF.
- FEEL YOURSELF ALREADY HAVING IT OR DOING WHAT YOU DESIRE. BREATHE THE SUGGESTION UP TO YOUR HIGHER SELF.
- FINISH THE SESSION BY TELLING THE LOW SELF IT IS COMPLETE.
- CUT YOUR CORDS SO YOU RELEASE YOUR DESIRES UP TO YOUR HIGHER SELF AND LET GO OF THE TIME IT WILL TAKE TO MANIFEST. BE THANKFUL THAT IT IS ALREADY DONE.

You may also recite the closing prayer to your Higher Self, said by the kahunas, "My prayer has now taken flight. Let the rain of blessings fall. It is finished."

Make sure that you always see yourself in the "desired form." Any negative thought or picture will confuse the unconscious mind and will stop the suggestion from reaching the Higher Self.

With these simple techniques outlined in this full chapter – the cutting of cords, the connection with the Higher Self, the chanting, the de-possession – you are on your way to uncover what has always been there. Make sure that you are ready to find your friggin' joy! Because … here it comes!

SECTION 4 – YOUR FRIGGIN' JOY

"Always forgive your enemies, nothing annoys them so much."

– Oscar Wilde

Chapter 19 – It's About Time

A ll of us have felt "extreme joy" at one time or another. Our team wins a coveted championship; our children make something special for us; we get acknowledged by our peers; we buy a new car or a new "bling," and the list goes on. Of course, we can't deny the joy we feel witnessing a glorious sunset, a field of brightly colored flowers, or hearing the high-pitched tones of wild dolphins under water. The unconditional love we receive from our pets is undeniable and fills the void inside on a continual basis. But what happens when the sunset disappears and the newness of the car or bling has died down, and we're home alone with our thoughts? Where is the joy then? Where has it gone? The truth is the joy that originated outside ourselves is only temporary. In order for a lasting experience of joy, we must secure the joy within.

Many years ago, I nurtured the idea that making a movie would finally fulfill a lifelong joyful dream. In 1993, I got a call from my agent to audition for the lead in a romantic erotica film by a renowned commercial and industrial filmmaker, Deborah Shames. She said there might be some artistic "nudity" and asked if I would be ok with that. Being European, my agent thought it to be no big deal. But it was to me. I had never even taken off my jacket or kissed on screen before. The roles I had already played were harmless, simple and conservative: a housewife in a Coit carpet cleaning commercial, an irate mother in an oral surgery film, a mother on the TV series *Midnight Caller*, a futuristic doctor in a Robin Williams' film, and various gigs as a precision stunt driver. When the casting director, Scott Fortier, called me directly and asked me to come in for the audition, I knew this was a big deal. It sparked my curiosity because in my early acting days I dreamed of being on a steamy, sexy, soap opera. It was obvious I had clearly passed the ingénue stage. Being 47 years old, I was flattered to even be considered for the part. What were they thinking? All those daily pushups and sit-ups at the gym were finally paying off. When I got a "call back" to read again, it became clear the part would have some nudity and a "hard R" rating.

Reality was finally hitting me. Casting me in the erotic romance movie *Cabin Fever* pushed me completely out of my comfort zone and into the "danger zone." Doing a love scene in front of a camera crew broke down a ton of barriers. The director would say, "Now your leg goes over there. When I count to three, suck her toe." Movie love scenes are choreographed! Not exactly a recipe for romance. My co-star and I connected in a deep way that was very natural. After all, we were both SAG actors who were very serious about our careers. The camera picked up on that authenticity, and this translated to our audience.

Critics loved the film. Gerald Nachman, renowned movie critic, gave us a full front-page article in the "Pink" section of the San Francisco Chronicle. The movie also got front-page display in the "Living" section of the San Jose Mercury News. This attention attracted a frenzy of reporters and talk-show hosts, all asking for guest appearances. There was a story in People Magazine, USA Today, feature stories on the TV show *Hard Copy,* and on CNN, to name a few. Much to my surprise, I was not as comfortable with all the attention as I thought I would be. Where was that "joy" I thought I would find with this experience? For some reason unknown to myself, I wanted to climb back into my shell and hide. What was this reaction about? I had been vulnerable on film and didn't like all the additional exposure in the public media. Dating was even more challenging because it seemed the men were interested in the character on the screen and not in the real person standing before them. I became very guarded.

My manager and agent encouraged me to believe that my acting career would continue to "build on this momentum" if I moved to Los Angeles. Following this advice, I leased a town house in Burbank while listing my Cupertino house for sale. Months passed and I didn't get a nibble on the house. It was getting increasingly difficult to maintain two mortgages.

Then I had a dream. In the dream I had fallen asleep beneath a large tree. The roots became the feet of an elephant and when I looked up, the tree was indeed an elephant dressed in regal robes and jewels and measuring as tall as a skyscraper. I heard the message, "Do not be afraid. All barriers will be gone." When I woke up, I knew exactly what to do. I was definitely not moving to Los Angeles. After making that decision, I got the money back from the lease in LA – a miracle in itself. One week later, an offer came in on my house and it sold. I moved to Tiburon and felt happy to continue my healing studies in Hawaii. Curious about that "elephant" in my dream, I learned that it was Lord Ganesha, the Hindu god that breaks down barriers. I was certainly conflicted about my choice of acting career over healing work. Spirit was guiding me towards the healing. The acting doors appeared locked for a reason. I believe that making the decision to become a healer and not an actress was a choice in the right direction, because this choice has allowed me the opportunity to help others and to heal myself.

With this story, I wish to show that when your soul is unhappy, it will let you know. Your outer life will reflect it. The barriers will pile up, as they did with me when my house didn't sell. As soon as I made the decision to stay in the Bay Area and not move to Los Angeles, the barriers came crashing down. Only YOU can take the first step. No one can do that for you. But as soon as you do, you can breathe a sigh of relief because then you get the loving support of your Higher Guides opening new doors that are more in alignment with your Highest Purpose. Go against that purpose and you will feel "heaviness," knowing deep down that something is not right. You might lose sleep and experience a lot of "mind chatter." Dis-ease may even take over your body. And you will not be joyous. You will miss that friggin' joy we are pursuing here.

I've always been curious about what makes people happy or joyous throughout their lives. I've seen that the happiest of people are the ones who can – even when disaster strikes – find gratitude in their heart for something. I remember a story from a Tony Robbins seminar. Tony asked this question during a Fortune 500 meeting: "How many of you feel really happy and successful?" Mind you, these people were all millionaires and very successful according to most people's standards. But Tony wanted to see if they really felt happy and successful. Only a handful of people raised their hands. One guy was jumping up and down and obviously felt inspired to speak. When Tony asked him why he was so excited, he said, "Every day above ground is a great day!" This man was in the Vietnam War, but he did not return in a body bag like a lot of his buddies. So every day "above ground" was joyful to him. It's as though he made it possible to win at the game of life.

Many people set the bar too high. Even though the majority of the people in the Fortune 500 meeting had huge bank accounts, they were not satisfied because they didn't have more money in the bank. If money is the goal, there will never be enough. If anything in the physical world is the goal, there can never be enough. But if the simple things in life are important, you will always find a way to be happy. My daughter Jessica, a 6th and 7th grade English and Drama teacher, revealed to me that she is joyful when she is creative. She is the most creative person I know. As a child, she designed clothes for her dolls out of toilet paper; as an adult she makes jewelry, sews, weaves, crochets, knits, cooks, bakes and writes poetry. To this day, the two poems she wrote for me are the most treasured joyful gifts I have received. The first one dedicated to me on my birthday, April 3, 1989.

The silver dew drops glisten, Upon the graceful limbs of trees.

The autumn leaves that fell are being pushed gently by the breeze.

But these beauties slowly dwindle into long, warm summer nights

As the beauty you project continues to grow bright.

As a child, I knew you only as my keeper.

Yet, now that I have grown, my feelings have grown deeper.

It is our destiny to live Life to its full extent

And with you by my side, we will live now as we're meant.

So another year has passed, But time means absolutely nada

For love and warmth combined make me glad that you're my mama!!!!

- Jessica Brooks (14 years)

The extreme joy I feel when I read this poem has only deepened as time goes by. Again, this time in 2004, Jessica surprised me with another soulful poem. This one entitled "Thinking of us on your Birthday."

"Not a day goes by I don't think of you. Nature breathes your name in soft whispers,

The artful glide of a monarch,

Impassioned flight of a hummingbird

Colors so vibrant, bright and living, the beat of my heart still vibrates with you

As if we are carrying each other.

So much have you given that I am full, spilling over –

Your love trails behind me like feathers,

Weightless and pulsing,

119

Murmuring angels and small chiming bells

Lift me over currents of sadness, loneliness,

Returning me to my spirit, to God, to you.

We are joined above time and space,

Bound by ribbons of mirrors and Light,

And I know you are always right –

I am protected by angels,

The spirit of God strong within me,

Your love unfailing, unyielding, forever, ever,

And mine for you. We carry each other.

Not a day goes by I don't think of you.

Nature breathes your name,

I am held again at your breast,

Safe, close, perfect.

"Thank you," I whisper back.

My daughter's words have cradled me and rocked me into the deepest sense of joyful calm that I have ever known. All the challenging years of raising children had their rewards after all. For it is the greatest gift to know you are appreciated by those you love.

So what makes you happy? Here is an exercise to find out.

1. List your talents and joyful endeavors even if they seem insignificant. What makes your heart sing? (Use the following page to write out your answers.)

2. On the following page, list out all those things for which you are grateful.

Upon filling out this page, you may want to reflect to see what it is that actually brings you joy and happiness. You may see what it takes to thrive on a mental, emotional and spiritual level, and to get the most out of life.

My mother, Consuelo, only picture of real father,
Patrick Michael Moore holding me. 1945

Working on Capitol Hill for Senator Charles
H. Percy, Washington D.C. 1967

Newspaper Review of "Cat's Paw" play, a Mastrosimone
thriller, City Lights Theatre Co. 1987

Fashion and Commercial Modeling Days, 1988

My daughter, Jessica Brooks and her
husband Edward Lee Brooks Jr.

Graduation from the Bob Bondurant High Performance
Driving Competition Road Racing course, 1988

Formula Ford Racing at Sears Pt. Raceway, Sonoma, Ca. 1989

Jumping for Joy at Sears Pt. Racetrack.

On Location shooting car commercials.

With Anthony Robbins at Certification
Program in Maui, Hi 1989

ACDelco Sparkplugs Commercial, Novato, Ca. 1990

San Jose Mercury News Entertainment Living Section.
About the film "Cabin Fever" 3/6/93

People Magazine Featured article about "Cabin Fever" 4/19/93

Reached the summit of Huayna Picchu,
Peru, Winter Solstice, 2000

Wild llama in Peru hears me chanting a
Hawaiian chant and gives me a kiss.

Komodo dragon stretches up to listen to
Hawaiian chants, Bali, 2001

Mother's Day in Santa Cruz. Jessica, baby Eddie, Brian, and me.

My son's college graduation from Cal State, Stanislaus 2008

On the Red Capet at the Screen Actors
Guild Awards Show, Jan. 2012

Huna Dolphin Adventure Retreat, the Big Island, Hi 2012

Huna, Level 1 Initiation, Kealakekua Bay, Hi
Kathleen Armstrong and Belinda, 2012

Belinda does Reconnective Healing on a horse in Hawaii. 2012

Chapter 20 — You
Already Have It All

Here is a story. A fisherman told a businessman that he had enough to support his family's immediate needs. The businessman then asked, "But what do you do with the rest of your time?" The fisherman said, "I sleep late, fish a little, play with my children, take walks with my wife, stroll into the village each evening where I sip wine and play guitar with my friends. I have a full and busy life." The businessman scoffed. "I am a Harvard MBA and could help you. You should spend more time fishing and with the proceeds, buy a bigger boat, and with the proceeds from the bigger boat you could buy several boats. Eventually you would have a fleet of fishing boats. Instead of selling your catch to a middleman, you would sell directly to the processor, eventually opening your own cannery. You would control the product, processing and distribution. You would need to leave this small coastal fishing village and move to the big city, where you will run your expanding enterprise."

The fisherman asked, "But, how long will this all take?" The businessman replied, "15-20 years."

"But what then?"

The businessman laughed and said that was the best part. "When the time is right you would announce an IPO and sell your company stock to the public and become very rich; you would make millions."

Said the fisherman, "Millions ... then what?"

The businessman said, "Then you would retire, move to a small coastal fishing village where you would sleep late, fish a little, play with your kids, take walks with your wife, stroll to the village in the evenings where you could sip wine and play your guitar with your friends."

This story says it all. Most of us have everything deep inside us to be joyful. It's the allure to the distractions in the world that seem to pull us away from the real treasures inside us. Amid all the environmental changes in the world – changes that have brought destruction and devastation by way of tornados, tsunamis and earthquakes – we continue to see people picking up the pieces of their lives and setting a new course. It seems that tragedy brings us together to reconnect and to help one another. The feeling of camaraderie connects us all.

Known as the world's oldest man, Walter Breuning, recently passed away at 114 in Great Falls, Montana. His secret to a long and joyful life was, "to keep using our mind and our body, eat only two meals a day, embrace change, even when the change slaps you in the face. Every change is good, work as long as you can, help others. The more you do for others, the better shape you're in. Never be afraid to die, because we're born to die." Walter would speak to his core group of friends in the nursing home. This kept him going, as he felt part of a big family. Money was not mentioned. It was important to provide the basics but not to expect a stockpile. What made him joyful was his connection to the people around him, giving him a sense of security and belonging. We all have a yearning to belong and be accepted. When this is present it makes our heart sing.

Chapter 21 – Taking Full Responsibility

This section is about the very necessary aspect of growth – taking full responsibility for your life ... your entire life.

Sylvia's son Chad (a man in his thirties) blames Sylvia for losing a fortune in an investment scheme. He yells and screams at her because now he will not receive the money he felt was "owed to him." Sylvia always paid her son's expenses, taking him on expensive vacations, and waiting on him hand and foot. Because of her divorce, she felt she had to take care of him even as an adult. You might ask yourself how this young man could expect such treatment. It's important to know that people needing love and approval will do whatever it takes to get it. Sylvia needed approval from her son to feel loved. The more she did for him, the more love she expected she would receive. Yet there was always that "hole in the pit of her stomach" after the high of providing what her son wanted. When the money stopped coming in, Sylvia could not provide for her son the way in which he had become accustomed. Of course, listening to him rant and rave at her after "all I have done for him" felt like a knife piercing her heart. At the very least, she can now see what doing all those things for her son helped co-create. With "learned helplessness" he became someone who was not capable of taking full responsibility for what life had dealt him.

Sylvia always took care of others before thinking about herself. As Sylvia battled with breast cancer, radiation and chemo, her energy depleted to the point of barely being able to take care of herself, something she didn't normally do. It is my belief that when you do not nurture yourself, then that nurturing part of a woman, the breasts, take on the illness. Sylvia will admit that she took care of others over herself all her life. She felt she had to "do things for others" to earn their love. In the final stages of her life, she finally realized that her past behavior was not working. She simply began to honor her own wishes, thus giving herself more love and feeling peaceful at last.

Life is all about learning lessons and accepting our second chances. How else can we learn the lessons unless we fail, not once, not twice, but as many times it takes to know when something isn't working? Once we see Plan A didn't work, we can go to Plan B.

Barbara blamed her parents for her miserable life. "They didn't bring me up to be successful," she declared tearfully. After using this excuse for a while and realizing that she didn't get the sympathy she felt she deserved, Barbara changed her thinking. Now she's in school learning the healing arts and admits that taking responsibility for her life is the only way she can make her life successful. "It's up to me," she says now. Visiting with her today, she looks more relaxed and happy.

During almost 20 years of providing healing and counseling to my clients, I have felt that the people who came to me were drawn to me to reach a higher purpose. One client in particular, John, told me, "I always knew I would be in a wheelchair." He remembers when he was younger observing several paralyzed victims and wondered how it would feel to be in "their place." When John was 19 years old he was in an automobile accident resulting in a broken neck. Just as expected, the accident put him in a wheelchair. Now 36 years later John comes to me for a Reconnective Healing session. During the session, I'm feeling, finding and stretching the frequencies around him that are the frequencies of his Higher Self. I don't have an agenda to give him anything specific in the healing. The more detached I am to the outcome, the more Light the client receives. He or she often receives something deeper than they expected. The higher frequencies know what John needs to heal at the deepest level of his being. As a result of the first session, John admitted to me that he finally forgave himself for his broken neck. He also admitted that now he feels "less of a victim." He says that by forgiving himself and not blaming others he feels a sense of empowerment. His freed-up energy is now focused on other endeavors that stimulate his enthusiasm for life.

After doing the official "Reconnection" – which takes place over a two-day period approximately 40 minutes each day – John is now beginning to see the possibility of walking again. He feels he is done with his karmic experience in "the chair" and can move out of this mindset, seeing and feeling himself hiking again. The purpose of The Reconnection is to accelerate you on your life path. It is only done once in a lifetime and connects you back to the axiatonal system of the Universe and the lay lines of the earth. (See Chapter 3.1.7 of *The Book of Knowledge: The Keys of Enoch* by J.J. Hurtak.)

After I completed my own Reconnection a few years ago, I knew I was supposed to write this book. I had been putting off writing it for the longest time. Finally, all the pieces came together to make it happen. I knew that it was directly related to becoming a Reconnective Healing Practitioner and doing The Reconnection. It accelerated me on the path of my Higher Self's calling for me. Recently, I heard a great quote, "Your career is what you get paid for. Your calling is what you're made for."

The feeling of taking full responsibility for our choices gives us a sense of empowerment. It's a sense that the direction we're taking is based on our soul's desire rather than our ego's desires. Guided to make choices that will enhance that direction, we feel profoundly supported. We make our own decisions based on a deep sense of "knowing" or intuition. And like the skipper of a ship, we steer our boat in the right direction and prepare to guide it through the storms of life.

Chapter 22 – The Path Before You

If you are moved to take action after reading this book, if you have followed along with the techniques and exercises as you read along, then the next steps are obvious. Practice, practice, practice. You are getting to know yourself now even deeper. Your decision to "clean house" will lighten your load and open you up to feeling friggin' joyful for no apparent reason. You might start hugging strangers for no reason at all. "Skipping therapy" may suddenly appear out of nowhere. Do not be alarmed. You won't be locked up … unless you want to be.

Deciding to "take responsibility" for your life will be a key element to bring empowerment to your life and to return to you the keys to a magic world. Be gentle with yourself. Rome wasn't built in a day, a week, or even a year. Your life is a masterpiece … and masterpieces take time. Developing new habits to clean yourself from the inside out will take about 21 days. It takes that long for the unconscious mind to know you are serious about fully embarking on this journey. You and your unconscious will work together as a team to reach your Higher Self. Enjoy the ride.

Chapter 23—"The Magic Inside"- Connecting the Missing Links

"And in the end, the love you take is
equal to the love you make."

- The Beatles

We began this journey, this book, with a quote nestled in a subtle way at the bottom of the Table of Contents. It was Mark Twain who said, "Forgiveness is the fragrance that the violet sheds on the heel that has crushed it." And throughout this text, as we have learned to dissolve cords with others, to perceive our brothers and sisters differently through our own self-forgiveness, to truly understand that forgiveness is actually about dissolving the way we are looking at someone or something, we have found our freedom and our joy. We have found the "missing links" required to truly forgive and be free. We have learned to truly "turn the other cheek" not in avoidance or feigned indifference, but as souls practicing true forgiveness – allowing people to do as they will, allowing life to happen as it will, knowing we can be just like the violet: spreading its natural fragrance despite the heel that has crushed it.

For we have learned well and with depth. As we forgive ourselves through the Higher Self, the cords of discord actually dissolve and become different energy. Everything is energy, not deemed good or bad, and as we transform so does the darkness of negative thought forms. We both become lighter as the weight is lifted from our hearts and the perceptions of the world are restored to its rightful view of beauty and grace.

Surprising to many of you perhaps, the art of forgiving others is the forgiving of ourselves for the perceptions and reactions we have of others. In reacting to and attaching to the negative actions of others, it's as if we are plugging an electric cord into a light socket. When we want revenge or carry a grudge, we are "plugged into" the emotion of revenge and enmity. The electric bill inside your body will carry you into deficit unless you unplug from the way you perceive them or their actions. Having to lower our own inner electric bill, we have decided to pull the plug, as we learned to do the HA breath, practice the Ho'oponopono process, connect with a Higher Self, and express honestly a unity that would say, "I forgive you," "I release you," "I love you." We have learned to, as it says in the Aramaic translation of the Lord's Prayer, "untie the tangled cords of destiny that bind us, as we release others from the entanglement of past mistakes."

The good news is – no matter what has happened to you in your life, no matter the pain or losses – THE JOY IS NOT LOST. That inner joy is simply hiding inside us, waiting to be discovered. Knowing that, would you BE READY to do whatever it takes to DISCOVER your JOY? Are you ready to feel happy for no apparent reason? You didn't earn it – YOU DESERVE IT! It is your birthright to advance your soul and lighten your load. "The Magic Inside" is your joy waiting to be uncovered. You don't have to be a magician to make this work. When you begin to discard the blanket surrounding your joy – when you brush off the plaque of your soul – by following the steps prescribed in this book, you will feel a lightness that is absolutely joyful. This book has taken you through some simple steps to get you started. Herein you learned of ancient Hawaiian healing secrets that are no longer hidden, the missing links that are no longer missing. Together with the frequencies of "The Reconnection," we have the recipe to advance to a higher dimension if we so choose. In my humble opinion, connecting to the Higher Self, an aspect we all possess, is the single most important endeavor you will accomplish in your lifetime.

Now that you know the secrets of uncovering the magic inside yourself... friggin' GO FOR IT! You got that? Nothing to lose. What are you waiting for? No time to waste. I wonder how surprised and amazed you will feel about yourself once that MAGIC inside you is revealed. What do you have to lose except your limitations? Your task is to dissolve the negative thought-forms accumulated in your lifetime that are draining you from creating new ideas in this present time. Thankfully, the cobwebs of your mind will dissolve by following the simple steps outlined for you in this book. Your willingness and faith in the process are the keys to getting started. No matter how forceful my words, no one can force you to start. It is my prayer that the information in this book provides the assistance you needed to FIND YOUR FRIGGIN' JOY.

Some may look forward on their journey and think it may be too hard or too long of a process. Get over it. Please don't allow the limitations of your mind to convince you otherwise. You read this book for a reason. Now get on with your purpose. In order to make the journey lighter, you can MAKE this adventure FUN. Ask yourself this question: "How can I begin this journey and enjoy the process?" Your mind will be guided to find a way to focus on "fun ways" and then discover how it can be. But you must first pose the question, hold the clear intention and be open and patient for the resulting answers. Along your path, you will also want to keep in mind seven important points of consideration. I offer them as a summary:

1. Connecting with your Higher Self is the ultimate gift you can give yourself.

2. Take responsibility for everything that happens to you in your life. Even if you unconsciously created it, you can then consciously un-create it.

3. Clean the pipeline to your Higher Self by cutting the cords or attachments from the past using the Forgiveness Process described in this book (and also on the CD *Chant and Forgiveness - A Huna Odyssey*). Continue to unplug your wires from the socket that feeds your "hot buttons." In

other words, keep cleansing yourself with the words, "I love you, I forgive you, thank you God." Feel the emotion of the words and not just the mental meaning. We shower and prep ourselves on the outside to look good to others; we can also develop the habit to prep and clean ourselves on the inside. As we stop shouldering the burdens of the past, we feel "lighter" and this translates into bringing to the surface more "joy."

4. Do conscious HA breathing throughout the day in sets of four to send the "mana" to your Higher Self. Because the Higher Self has no body, it needs the accumulated energy and breath generated by the unconscious mind from your physical body. It can use that positively charged energy to assist in granting our prayers in our physical reality. The Higher Self cannot manifest our desires without fuel from our physical body provided by our Unconscious Mind. Don't be a "ha-ole" – one without breath. It takes 21 days to make a habit. So you must do conscious HA breathing until it becomes unconsciously part of your daily ritual. You can do this anywhere – sitting at your desk, driving your car, waiting in line at the post office, etc.

5. FORGIVE YOURSELF from the past no matter what. Wipe the slate clean … for the good of you, those you may have harmed and all you touch in your life.

6. Practice GRATITUDE. Find something for which you feel grateful, even when it seems there is nothing to be grateful for.

7. Do something PLAYFUL every day. LAUGH FOR NO REASON.

In creating this summary chapter, I find it vital to let you know that accepting ourselves as we are does not mean that we are our thoughts or our beliefs. We can accept and embrace aspects of ourselves and still not solely identify with them. In fact the very idea that we can embrace them proves that we are something bigger and more expansive than these beliefs and limitations. Underneath our ego's judgment of us lies the pure beauty of our Soul, waiting for redemption and the freedom to love, create and just BE.

We must all be willing to allow ourselves to let go in our adventure of uncovering that soul and finding that joy, just like the pirates of old used to go for the great treasures. Can YOU be the pirate in your own treasure hunt discovering the fountain of your own true self, which is the real "Fountain of Youth?" I'll bet that you're starting to get excited realizing all the possibilities!

That excitement is what I want to trigger in you, as it has been revitalized in me. When I was a little girl, I was taken to see the play *Peter Pan*, and was astonished to see this young lad fly across the stage. The music always inspired me not to take myself too seriously and to add a "playful dimension" to my life. Pure inspiration comes from the Higher Self. The words from this song in particular, remind me of discovering the magical connection to our Higher Self:

I have a place where dreams are born and time is never planned.

It's not on any chart — You must find it with your heart — Never Never Land.

It might be miles beyond the moon, or right there where you stand.

Just keep an open mind. And then suddenly you'll find — Never Never Land.

You'll have a treasure if you stay there, far more precious than gold.

For once you have found your way there...

You can never, never grow old.

For it is true, living in the past ages us. Living in the present embraces us. Whatever you choose, be gentle with yourself. As you get to know yourself even deeper, you will marvel at the pure love that walks with you. In the words of Marcus Aurelius, "Look within. Within is the fountain of good, and it will ever bubble up, if thou wilt ever dig." As a fellow traveler on this sacred journey, I wish that your heart be as light as a feather.

It will take all of us, coming from that enlightened heart, to usher in a new world. And what will this new world hold for us? Our joy. Our friggin' joy.

That is the key. It has always been the key. When you find your inner connection you will reside in the present time. It is here you see possibilities. The past will be gone, and once it is, you are in the present moment – you are in the joy. Right now. It's in the present moment that you can create something anew, with all hope and all possibilities before you.

And what does that feel like? Amazing. It's absolutely giggly ... a feeling just as precious as a **Sunflower** or the ocean view or the dawning Sun. You feel so happy to be alive. You have another chance to breathe, another chance to love, another chance to create. And once you have it for yourself, you have another chance to assist others in finding their joy.

It's true we've lost our joy throughout time. We've accumulated all this inner plaque and constructed all these illusions around us that steal away that joy. Our mortgages, gas prices, Wall Street, car payments and "keeping up with the Joneses." You can't be joyful there. Yes, of course you have to make a living, but making a living doesn't have to create a poison in your life to rob you of your joy. The more things you accumulate, the more you can get lost in them. Sometimes by losing so much, you can find what is really there in your life. **You.**

I recently saw a movie *Everything Must Go*. In it, the lead character was an alcoholic whose wife kicked him out of the house and threw all his stuff on the front lawn. So that's where he lived: the front lawn. And in that process of letting go, he finally found his core, as he shed everything he had and learned to start life over – with just an identity stripped away from everything he thought defined him.

Throughout my own life, I have found when I lost some things that didn't define me; I discovered who I really was at the core. I found how little those things contributed to who I am. It wasn't until I lost all my money and until the travesty of losing my son, that I was scraped to the bottom. It wasn't until all I was holding on to was gone that I found there was something else there. Through a committed journey using the healing tools outlined in this book, I was able to find my friggin' joy: that ironically illusive element of our lives that never truly leaves us. I found out that when you have nothing else but yourself, you have to go inside, and face who you are. And it happens: you find out who you really are.

And here is the good news. You are brilliance. **You are the sunflower, the joy.** You are a pearl in an oyster waiting to be discovered. You are worthy. You deserve. You are a child of God, a child of the Universe. You are here now to advance your soul and lighten your load. You are unburdening your heart from the past, and the guilt, and the loss, and the things of this world. And you are doing so in order to find your true love.

What I have discovered is we all end up finding we are in love with love itself, with a self that is truly defined as love. For we are the relationship we've been waiting for, in a relationship with our true selves.

In completing this book, I'm befuddled how I was even able to do it. I'm not really a writer as much as a healer and a speaker. But through the process, I have done what I set out to do. With a heart full of gratitude, I wished to assist people, give them a kick in the pants, give them a boost, and give them hope. I hope that I have done this. The entire purpose to write this book was to share my journey in hopes that other people would see themselves in that journey and free themselves to find the love within--to find that relationship for which they have been searching for a lifetime.

May you enjoy the "bumpy" ride as you complete your soul's purpose.

Forgiveness is the Key!
Freedom lies Within,
Find Your Friggin' Joy...
And CELEBRATE your WIN!
Boundless peace and joy to you all.

About the Author

As a Certified Master Hypnotherapist, NLP Master Practitioner, Huna Practitioner, and Reconnective Healing Practitioner, Belinda Farrell is effective at getting results and enhancing performance for her clients. She graduated from the University of California at Berkeley with a B.A. in English and Spanish. After obtaining a Lifetime Elementary Teaching Credential at Cal State LA, she taught third grade for five years in Puerto Rico and Los Angeles. She played the character Snow White at Disneyland, held a position as TV News Reporter for KABC Channel 7 in Hollywood and worked on the staff of Senator Charles H. Percy (Illinois) in Washington, D.C.

Belinda trained with Anthony Robbins (author of *Unlimited Power* and *Awaken the Giant Within*), and has effectively used these skills in her own life. In addition to fire walking, (18 times), Belinda has tested the limits as a professional Precision Stunt Car Driver for TV commercials and films. Her credits include ads for Buick, Cadillac, BMW, Volvo, Nintendo, Audi, Toyota, Lexus, AC Delco Spark Plugs and many more. She was a film and stage actress, having co-starred on the TV series *Midnight Caller*, in addition to making dozens of industrial films, commercials and voice-overs. As a mother and grandmother, Belinda Farrell loves to workout, rollerblade, snow ski, and simply lives a healthy life, having as much fun as possible.

.

RESOURCES AND FURTHER CONNECTIONS

BOOKS

CHILES, Pila (Pila of Hawaii), *The Secrets & Mysteries of Hawaii*, Health Communications, Inc. Deerfield Beach, Florida. *God-Link, Is There a Higher Plan for Humanity?* (*www.MysticalHawaii.com*)

GLOVER, William R. *Huna, The Ancient Religion of Positive Thinking*, Huna Press, 126 Camellia Dr., Cape Girardeau, MO 63701 1979

HAY, Louise, *Heal Your Body,* Hay House, 1984

JAMES, Tad (with George Naope & Rex Shudde), *Lost Secrets of Ancient Hawaiian Huna – 1*

LONG, Max Freedom, *Growing Into Light, A Personal Guide to Practicing the Huna Method*, DeVorss Publications, 1955

LONG, Max Freedom, *The Secret Science at Work, The Huna Method as a Way of Life,* DeVorss Publications, 1953

LONG, Max Freedom, *What Jesus Taught in Secret*, Huna Press, Cape Girardeau, MO, 1978

LONG, Max Freedom, *Recovering the Ancient Magic*, Huna Press, 1978

MELCHIZEDEK, Drunvalo, *The Ancient Secret of the Flower of Life*, Vol. 1, Light Technology Publishing, Flagstaff, AZ 86003, (800) 450-0985

MYSS, Caroline PhD, *Why People Don't Heal and How they Can*, Three Rivers Press, New York (Reference: *Snow White and the Seven Chakras*)

ROBBINS, Anthony, *Unlimited Power* and *Awaken the Giant Within*, Amazon.com

WILDE, Stuart, *The Little Money Bible* (The Ten Laws of Abundance), Hay House, Carlsbad, CA, 1998

INFORMATION ON RECONNECTIVE HEALING
TheReconnection.com
BELINDA FARRELL'S WEBSITE
HunaHealing.com
CONTACT
Belinda Farrell
415 250-8094
BelindaFarrell44@Yahoo.com
Management
Jennifer Geronimo of Life Enlightenment
(619) 713-6756
JMGeronimo@AOL.com

Other Available Resources from Belinda Farrell

CD'S available from NEW LEAF DISTRIBUTORS, <u>www.hunahealing.com</u>, and amazon.com

1. **CHANT and FORGIVENESS...A HUNA ODYSSEY** first released 1995

    (Ho'oponopono- A closed eye forgiveness process)
2. **EnCHANTment...Ancient Hawaiian Chants to the Higher Self** 2003 (A Higher Self Connection together with sounds of dolphins & whales) 8 page booklet with the chants included.
3. **SLEEPY TIME CHANT** 2005 (Ancient Hawaiian Dream Chant for Relaxation, Meditation or Sleep)

    MP3 format from <u>www.hunahealing.com</u> and iTunes

HEALING SERVICES by BELINDA FARRELL
Belinda conducts **RECONNECTIVE HEALING SESSIONS** in person or by long distance. Typically, these sessions are 30-40 minutes in length. The healings occur outside of the constraints of time and space so additional time is not necessary. One to three sessions are recommended.

Belinda also does THE RECONNECTION which consists of two sessions IN PERSON, generally 45 minutes to one hour or so in length, and ideally on consecutive or alternate days. This is only done **once** in your lifetime.

HUNA TRAINING (levels 1,2,3,4) see website: www.hunahealing. com conducted in Santa Cruz, California, and on The Big Island of Hawaii, with wild dolphin adventures.

Contact sheet for Modern Day Visionaries

1. **Scott Andrews**, founder of <u>www.AspireNow.com</u> Author, Speaker.

2. **Scott Burr** and **Dayna Hubenthal**, Publishers, Clackamus, Or. <u>burrs@kohopono.com</u>

3. **Celeste Eaton**, Dolphin guide on Big Island, Hi and Whales of Tonga. <u>www.celestialsonics.com</u>

4. **James Anthony Ellis**, owner of Legacy Productions in San Diego. Author, Producer, Videographer <u>www. LegacyProductions.org</u>

5. **Dr. Carol Francis**, Clinical Psychologist, Marriage and Family and Child Therapist. <u>www.doctorcarolfrancis.com</u>

6. **Doug Hackett** and **Tris Regan**, Big Island, HI. <u>www. dolphinspiritofhawaii.com</u>

7. **Francene Hart**, Visionary Artist, Big Island, HI. <u>www. francenehart.com</u>

8. **Broderick Perkins**, Executive Editor, San Francisco Bay Area <u>www.DeadlineNews.com</u>

9. **Dr. Cynthia Quattro**, Physician Assistant and Doctor of Acupuncture and Oriental Medicine, Soquel, Ca. Email:quattrodoc@gmail.com <u>www.drquattro.com</u>

10. **David Samson**, author, speaker, comedian and "Ad" man www.Adville.com

11. **Len Saputo, M.D., Orinda, Ca.** Co-author of "A *Return to Healing, Radical Health Care Reform and the Future of Medicine*" healthmedicine@comcast.com

12. **Shelley Stockwell, PhD**, President of International Hypnosis Federation www.hypnosisfederation.com

13. **James Wanless, PhD**, Creator of *Voyager Tarot* www.voyagertarot.com